I have known Pope Leo as mentor, as guide, as companion at the table in our refectory and at the table of the Lord. He has been a diligent listener, a considered responder, a provocateur for goodness and reason. But most of all he has always shown his care and love for those who have encountered him. His faith is expressed in actions, and only then backed up by words—a true son of Augustine.

Fr Anthony Banks, OSA
Assistant General for the Asia Pacific
Order of St Augustine

This little gem of a book builds on the excitement that electrified the world when Pope Leo XIV was chosen. Even as it names the monumental challenges he faces, what shines through is the character of a proven builder of bridges and apostle of peace, fuelling our hopes that by the grace of God he can bring about the transformation for which we so long.

Sr Barbara E Reid, OP
President of Catholic Theological Union
Chicago

Pope Leo XIV, An Apostle of Peace, Robert Francis Prevost has taken on the attention of the world within a brief period of time in his early Pontificate. An American whose origins reflect ordinary beginnings is now leading the Church on an extraordinary journey. This book will capture the reader's imagination.

Fr Anthony Benedetto Pizzo, OSA
Prior Provincial of the Province of the Midwest Augustinians
Chicago

This 'hot off the press' biography of our new Pope Leo XIV fills many of the gaps. The American Augustinian Robert Prevost with Peruvian citizenship was not listed as *papabile*, and yet in hindsight, he, and perhaps he alone, ticked all the boxes. Author Samuel Prevot was there in the square as the white smoke rose. Author Marc Leboucher, a good friend of Cardinal Barbarin, had access to the cardinals including Prevost over a meal just before the conclave began. These French authors have collaborated from Chicago, to Peru, and to the Vatican giving us vital first hand accounts of our new pope who will further the Francis commitment to the peripheries while consolidating the unity of the Church. As well as riveting eye witness accounts of the unfolding events of the conclave and the new papacy, they give us expert commentary including the insight that the papacy has moved from theocracy to influence and now to enunciating fundamental principles on the organisation of our world.

Fr Frank Brennan SJ AO
Adjunct Professor of Law, Australian Catholic University

I was delighted to read the drafts of this timely biography on Pope Leo XIV. The insights from the authors' conversations with Cardinal Barbarin and Sr Nathalie Becquart (in particular) were exceptionally informative; revealing aspects of the French Catholic Church and its remarkable contribution to Synodality—the great work of Pope Francis, and now Pope Leo XIV. While the work originates from France, and reflects the particular concerns of the French Catholic Church, it is also deeply enlightening for the universal church as we try to understand this new papal era.

Noel James Debien
Senior Specialist Producer,
ABC Compass, ABC Religion and Ethics

Pope Leo XIV

Samuel Prevot with Marc Leboucher

Pope Leo XIV

An Apostle of Peace

Samuel Pruvot with Marc Leboucher and I.Media.

Translated by Martin Wallace OP

Adelaide
2025

Publishers note: Pope Leo XIV was elected on the 8th of May 2025. The original French language edition of the book by Salvator was released on the 14th of May 2025. With a release date so soon after the election, some details of the text needed to be confirmed by ATF Press. In a number of instances, small changes have been made in the English edition. The Publisher takes responsibility for any changes from the original French text. The Introduction by Fr Tony Banks OSA was not in the original French text.

ISBN

978-1-923385-42-9	soft cover
978-1-923385-43-6	hard cover
978-1-923385-44-3	Epub
978-1-923385-45-0	PDF

Published by:

Making a lasting impact
An imprint of the ATF Press Publishing Group
owned by ATF (Australia) Ltd.
PO Box 234
Brompton, SA 5007
Australia
ABN 90 116 359 963
www.atfpress.com

Contents

Introduction

The election of Robert Cardinal Prevost OSA as our Holy Father and the new Bishop of Rome has been received with great joy by Augustinians and the greater Augustinian family across the world. I was fortunate to be in Rome for the white smoke emanating from the chimney atop the Sistine Chapel and to hear the name of our confrere proclaimed to the world. My travels two days later then took me to West Papua, a part of our Asian world where Indonesia became the second country to have an indigenous Asian Augustinian bishop ordained in service of the people It was Bob Prevost who had ensured the development of the Order in Africa and Asia during his terms as Prior General.

I had encountered Bob when he was a student but I came to know him particularly well during his two terms as Prior General of our Order. As a provincial counselor in Australia, I found him most helpful in referring me to materials that looked at the renewal of the Order when I worked in our province to help examine its future directions. He was well acquainted with materials from both Latin America and Spain during a period when our English-speaking circumscriptions were not yet developing their own plans for renewal. He also provided me with further links from the Chicago Province for materials on the development of an Augustinian parish.

Under his guidance the Order renewed our Constitutions. This second reworking post Vatican II made even more concrete the charisms and gifts of the Order and delineated better our role, as contemplatives in action, within the Church. The values of interiority, of truth, of holding all things in common were strengthened under the watchful gaze of a pastoral canon lawyer.

Previous Priors General were travellers but Robert Prevost was exceptional. As well as attending the circumscriptional Chapters of the Order held every four years in our many Provinces and Vicariates he also attended the Regional gatherings of friars in leadership. He was generally very gracious but could also be demanding where he saw individuals or groups deviating from the Rule of St Augustine or the Constitutions. His challenges were always presented as a means to grow and develop as an Order. And as a traveller he was able to alight after a long journey and commence his greetings and work as though as fresh as a daisy.

As Prior General Bob placed a great deal of emphasis on the outreach and growth of the Order in Africa and then in Asia. General Chapters were devoted to the recognition of these newer missions, so that now they provide missionaries back to the first world. In Asia he oversaw the development of the Order in South Korea for a number of years before turning it the Province of Australasia. He witnessed the continual growth of the Order in the Philippines and was the one who nominated two Filipinos as Asian Assistant General during his two terms of office. His was a familiar face at the conferences of the Augustinian leaders in Asia-Pacific (OSAAP) and of the leaders (male and female) of the greater Augustinian family in Asia-Pacific (APAC).

He further worked to strengthen the development of the Order from the Asia Pacific region by offering scholarships for further studies in Rome to members of the Order and by offering bursaries for studying at the Patristic Institute to Churches in Asia that needed assistance.

It is with special joy that I recall among his visits to Australia his presence at the Augustinian Youth Encounter, following World Youth Day 2008. There he spent time with the 300+ young men and women, and Augustinians, who had travelled to Australia for World Youth Day. This event hosted by the Australian province and the youth ministries within the Province was concluded with a Mass overlooking Collaroy beach where the now 'new Peter' was truly a fisherman of the people proclaiming the Johannine story of 'feeding my lambs, feeding my sheep'.

I have known Pope Leo as mentor, as guide, as companion at the table in our refectory and at the table of the Lord. He has been a diligent listener, a considered responder, a provocateur for goodness and reason. But most of all he has always shown his care and love for those who have encountered him. His faith is expressed in actions, and only then backed up by words—a true son of Augustine.

Anthony Banks, OSA
Assistant General for the Asia Pacific
Order of St Augustine
Rome
June 2025

Foreword

First lunch at Santa Martha

On 9 May 2025, Rome awoke still buzzing with excitement from the previous day's election of the new Pope Leo XIV. Having travelled with my colleagues from Salvator to prepare a book about him, I joined thousands of people in watching for the white smoke. At first, there were just a few wisps rising into the sky here and there, at first it was difficult to distinguish them from clouds. And yet, we had to believe it. *Habemus papam!*

But this Friday, unlike any other, I had an appointment at around 1 pm with my friend Cardinal Philippe Barbarin. 'Come and meet me at the Santa Marta guesthouse,' he told me on the phone. He took part in the conclave over the last few days and has just come out of the first Mass with the Holy Father in the Sistine Chapel. After negotiating with the Swiss guards, passing through security, and waiting under the blazing sun, I found him in the heart of the Vatican. The prelate greeted me with his warm smile and slowly led me to the dining room. The premises are vast, marble is everywhere; yet I feel as if I am in a small group. There is nothing solemn about it, except for the walls. And then, I am the only lay person, French at that, among some thirty cardinals from all over the world. Everyone helps themselves to the buffet and raw vegetables in a very informal manner. There is no stuffy protocol. With Philippe Barbarin, I sit down at a table with prelates from Madagascar, India, Thailand and Italy. We exchange a few personal memories, including that of another surprise election in 2013: that of Pope Francis.

Salad, the inevitable pasta, fish because it's Friday. Then a door opens, we stand up, applause breaks out. It is Leo XIV entering with a small entourage. No protocol here either: the cardinals welcome him as one of their own. The pope then makes his way around the tables, and my friend Philippe introduces me to him. 'I am a French religious publisher, Holy Father', I say in English. The retort comes quickly: 'Then you will be able to tell me the origin of my grandfather's name!' It is true that this American from the United States, who spent time in Peru, has the very French name of Prevost, like some inhabitants of my family's Berry region, not far from Bourges. 'I don't know the origin of that name yet, Holy Father.' 'Then you'll have to look for it!' he replies cheerfully. The audience laughs heartily. I add that we are preparing a book about him. He looks at me a little incredulously, then gives me a beautiful, encouraging smile. We pose for photos, including the one that appears on the cover of this book. Then I wish him good luck in his ministry. His gaze pierces me once more before he too goes to help himself at the buffet.

'Seek and ye shall find!' I cannot help thinking of this quote from the Gospel as I return to my table. I look at Leo XIV sitting a few metres away. Irresistibly, his slender silhouette reminds me of Paul VI. An elegance full of finesse, a patrician air. This man, who is said to be reserved, speaks naturally with his neighbours at the table. Shortly afterwards, mobile phones come out and many cardinals take photos with him. Memories must be preserved. There is Cardinal Marx, a specialist in social doctrine, with a predestined name; Cardinal Vesco OP, the Archbishop of Algiers, in his Dominican habit; Timothy Radcliffe OP, with his British humour, who assures me that he 'slept well last night' when I ask him for his impression of the election.

I will cherish the memory of this first lunch at Santa Marta for a long time to come.

'Seek and ye shall find!' This is also, in essence, the approach taken in the book you hold in your hands. It was written largely by my friend Samuel Pruvot and is the first biography of the new pope to be published in French. After many sleepless nights, the author paints a complete portrait of Leo XIV, recounting his election and career, the pressing issues that await him and the reactions to his appointment. It provides a wealth of information about the man who is now at the head of the Church.

In accepting this responsibility, Leo XIV, an Augustinian friar, perhaps remembered the opening words of the *Confessions* of his beloved Saint Augustine: 'You have made us for yourself, Lord, and our hearts are restless until they rest in you.'

Marc Leboucher
Literary Director at Salvator

1.

Habemus Papam!

Saint Peter's Square, 8 May, 6:08 p.m. *Fumata! Bianca!* White smoke billows from the Sistine Chapel, announcing the election of a new pope to succeed Francis. The clamour is immense. It brings to mind that fantastic passage from the Book of Revelation where the seer describes humanity saved: 'After this I looked, and there was a great multitude, which no one could count, a multitude from every nation, from all tribes and peoples and languages' (Rev 7:9).

The 133 cardinal electors gathered in conclave since Wednesday afternoon, 7 May, have voted. It was a very quick conclave: less than two days. In the fourth round of voting, as was the case twenty years ago for the election of Benedict XVI, the cardinals agreed on a name. The excitement is at its peak.

Fumata bianca. White smoke, which is very abundant, lingers for several minutes while a muffled deafening sounds starts to fill the air in the square. A blast of grace, a roar of joy that spreads like a wave to Castel Sant'Angelo and beyond. Pilgrims and onlookers continue to flock, trying to make their way through the dense crowd that had been waiting for the appearance of the new pope since mid-afternoon.

Two young women from Poland stare at the screens. They come from Przemysl, on the border with Ukraine. Ela, 20, and Beata, 34, are both Catholics. The say that 'Our pilgrimage to Rome was booked a month in advance . . . This morning we visited the Vatican Museum. We are waiting to find out who will be the next head of the Church, such an important position as pope . . . Because he is our guide. He has the authority to tell the world what is good and what is bad.'

Showing great joy, Bishop Jean-Yves Riocreux, emeritus bishop of the diocese of Basse-Terre in Guadeloupe, crosses the square jumping up and down. The French prelate is almost dancing, like King David, in front of the wall of cameras erected at the top of the Via della Conciliazione. The bishop fixes his eyes on the white smoke and with his feet, stamping like a child can be heard to say: 'Only four ballots! That is as fast as it was for Benedict XVI! You willl see, he's a man of consensus, a heavyweight chosen by the cardinals.'

Right next to him, two Iraqi nuns start waving their Iraqi flags. They are Dominican Sisters of Saint Catherine of Siena. They shout at the top of their voices: '*Viva! Viva!*' They have high hopes for the next pope who is about to appear in the loggia because they live in Karakoch, in a land ravaged by war. 'He is the head of the Church, it is so important for the future and for peace . . .'

At exactly 6:12 pm the bells of the basilica ring out at full volume. There is pure, childlike, and eschatological joy. Like a deliverance after a long period of underground and spiritual work in which more than a billion Catholics have participated in secret. The crowd is very eager to know the name and face of Francis' successor . . . the future and peace . . .

There is silence everywhere. After several long minutes of waiting, the white curtains of the loggia, the central balcony of the balcony of St Peter's Basilica, flutter. Monsignor Dominique Mamberti, a French cardinal, appeared. In an astonishing silence, he pronounced the famous words: *Annuntio vobis gaudium magnum: habemus papam* ('I announce to you great joy: we have a pope').

In St Peter's Square, a little angel wants to get out of his pram. He too wants to see what is happening on the loggia, where a modest white dot is attracting everyone's attention. Gabriel, a blond boy with blue eyes, looking like one of the angels from the Sistine Chapel, is stamping his feet with impatience. Colombe and Tanguy, his parents, had planned to come to Rome on a pilgrimage for the Jubilee. '6 May', adds Tanguy, 'is the anniversary of the sack of Rome in 1527, when nearly 150 Swiss Guards gave their lives to protect Pope Clement VII.' A former Swiss Guard himself between 2018 and 2020 and a newlywed, Tanguy was invited by the commander to attend the commemorative ceremony on 6 May. The ceremony was cancelled due to the Pope's death. 'A conclave was even better!' Colombe rejoices. 'We were having coffee right next door, at Porta Angelica, when we heard the incredible sound of the crowd! We started running towards St Peter's Square with the pram.' Colombe and Tanguy are accompanied by a good Italian friend. Maria Aurelia, 30, a true Roman: 'I came to see my new bishop! For me, it's a very special moment. Ever since I was little, I've attended all the major ceremonies with the popes. I have so many memories . . . How exciting to be able to see the new bishop of Rome soon!' As an Italian, Maria Aurelia embraces her deeply Catholic identity: 'We carry the weight of history with us here. I expect the pope to strengthen the faith of Catholics and confirm us in the truth. This point is very important to me. Faith must be a light for the whole world.'

A young Franciscan friar, Brother Luis, stands in the square. He has come to Rome on pilgrimage with other friars from his Order and shares his thoughts with us: 'I feel immense gratitude for Pope Francis. I hope there will be continuity. He has emphasised the importance of mercy so strongly.'

The sun plays on Bernini's columns. It is no doubt preparing for the appearance of the new pope. Stanislas, at the ripe old age of eight, can hardly wait any longer. 'It is very important: we're going to have a new pope!' explains the young French boy. 'It will go down in history. I hope we get a French pope. But I know there could also be Italian, Portuguese or a Swedish pope . . .' 'And why not an American?' Stanislas concludes thoughtfully: 'The pope is taking a long time to arrive because he must be a little scared. There are so many people waiting for him in this square . . .' Hugues, Stanislas's dad, is full of enthusiasm: 'We arrived from Paris last night. We are lucky! My favourite pope is John Paul II. We need bulls to charge ahead.' A bull or a lion—a 'Leon', etymologically speaking.

2.

The Birth of the Conclave

Let us go back a little. It is 24 April in the Vatican, in the middle of Eastertide, in the light of the Resurrection and the new life brought by Christ. The Church is preparing to enter a hopeful new phase, with the prospect of welcoming a successor to Peter. As Cardinal François Bustillo, who is participating in his first conclave, says, 'the work of the cardinals in the conclave is to give birth to a new pope'.

The third meeting between the cardinals is scheduled to take place early in the morning, and the numerous journalists—united in a single pack armed with microphones and cameras—are waiting eagerly at the Petrine gate leading to the Paul VI Hall. Each red cap tries as best it can to make his way through, sometimes uttering a few quick words as he passes. The cardinals eagerly await these 'general congregations' to get to know each other better before the big day, 7 May, the official date for the start of the conclave. During the *congregazioni generali*, each cardinal—whether an elector or not—is invited to take the floor to share his vision of the Church. Each has just a few minutes to speak. But history has shown that some speeches can hit the mark, tipping the balance of the assembled cardinals.

First Steps

Among the 135 cardinal electors expected in Rome—133 will ultimately vote—is, of course, the future pope. Vatican experts compete to compile lists of potential candidates, known as the '*papabili*'. They try in vain to predict the outcome of this human-divine election in the Sistine Chapel. 'Getting inside a cardinal's head is no easy task,' confides Hugues Lefèvre, director of I.Media, the Vatican Press Agency. 'A Vatican expert, with his rational criteria, cannot fully grasp the mystery of the choice that will be made.' It is a mystery that also captivates the bookmakers: 'The guessing game surrounding the *papabili* is fun, even exciting, but always risky and inevitably imprecise', warns Romilda Ferrauto, special advisor to the Holy See's press office.

Be Prepared for Anything

According to Cardinal Barbarin, we must be prepared for anything: 'The situation is very open. Since Francis, we have really moved into a different realm from a theological and geographical point of view. He has not been a pope like his predecessors. This is a beneficial renewal for the Church.'

How to choose a pope? A decision in which human criteria are important but not always decisive, insists Cardinal Bustillo: 'We are not going to look first at his passport or his political sensibilities. We are not going to ask ourselves if he is a nice person! We are not going to implement electoral tactics. To think in these terms would be to profane the conclave.' A serious reflection, but one that does not advance the predictions of Vatican experts one iota.

The Impossible Sketch of the Pope

A conclave is unlike any other election. So many human and spiritual factors come into play that only God can make sense of it. Now that the cardinals are preparing to lock themselves away, entrusted to the Holy Spirit, those outside are wondering who will be able to manage the sometimes explosive legacy of Pope Francis' pontificate. No doubt a cardinal compatible with Bergoglio? 'Not necessarily', jokes Cardinal Barbarin. 'Popes succeed one another and are not alike. Between John Paul II and Benedict XVI, there was a theological affinity, but no similarity in temperament. Between Benedict XVI and Francis, there was neither theological proximity nor similarity of character.'

During the congregations, there is still time to wonder what criteria could tip the balance in the College of Cardinals. Age, geographical origin, theological orientation, temperament: everything seems important. But to what extent? Romilda Ferrauto paints a portrait of a pope of synthesis: 'The electors could be attracted to a more spiritual figure, a leader capable of offering not only solutions to the Church's internal problems, but also a prophetic vision. In this sense, the challenge could be to successfully bring together institution and spirituality, doctrine and real life, tradition and innovation.' In short, what is occurring is 'squaring the circle'.

She sums up the situation as follows: 'Statistically speaking, it is likely that the next pope will be a cardinal appointed by Francis himself, but that does not mean he will be a Francis II. After all, Bergoglio was made a cardinal by John Paul II, but his pontificate was very different from that of the Polish pope. The conservative—progressive divide, which has certainly become more pronounced during this pontificate, will not necessarily have a decisive influence on the outcome of the next conclave.'

Romilda Ferrauto, on the other hand, points out that the geographical and cultural diversity of the electors could carry more weight than their ideological orientation. 'By renewing the College of Cardinals, Francis has given a voice to local churches that are often overlooked, broadening the representation of Asia, Africa and America.'

Listening to the Holy Spirit

On the evening of 24 April, the temperature continues to rise in Rome. No doubt this is due to the effects and speculation of Vatican journalists, whose minds are already in overdrive. How will they hold out until the day the white smoke appears? On the steps of the Church of St Louis of the French in Rome, Cardinal Jean-Claude Hollerich, General Relator of the synod and Archbishop of Luxembourg, answers questions from French-speaking journalists.

The Cardinal does not deny the plurality of viewpoints within the assembly.

> 'There are certainly very different visions, but that does not mean that the Church is "divided". We are in deeper communion than the opinions that divide us. At the synod, we were able to overcome divisions and avoid radicalism while maintaining the radicalism of the Gospel. It would be good to do the same and find common ground where we can walk together. Being conservative or progressive is not important. What is important is to have faith in the living Christ.'

Faith in Christ, but also in the Holy Spirit, a key player in the conclave: 'We trust in the Holy Spirit to decide! I am not the Holy Spirit! That doesn't mean we don't feel a certain apprehension, because we feel very small. We have to make decisions for the whole Church, so we really have to pray for us, so that we may listen to the Holy Spirit.'

For Cardinal Hollerich, the pope must first and foremost be a 'unifier, because Peter is the minister of unity in the Church.' He must also be able to think about young people. 'In our European countries, they will be poorer in the future than they are now. We have always lived in a world that [tended toward] the best, but they will experience the opposite. In addition to the threat of war, which has never been there for my entire personal history, there are also many rapid changes.' But this unifier, who must be 'neither too young nor too old', will have to behave like a man who listens.

> 'A simple man who can be in in touch with people, who knows how to listen to people, on the left and on the right. A pope who lives the Gospel, who represents face of Christ to the whole world. It is difficult to find. But I think God will also give the future pope a special grace . . . I believe in the Holy Spirit, and I know my limits. The Holy Spirit will not make a mistake.'

The Conclave, a Spiritual Adventure

The general congregations could nevertheless lack spiritual inspiration. 'The opening and closing prayers were rushed through', lamented one cardinal. 'We didn't even have time to stand up before the sign of the cross had already been made.'

Some have therefore sought peace elsewhere. An African cardinal chose to reside in the generalate of his religious order on the outskirts of Rome to prepare himself in prayer and reading the Gospels. 'I wanted to live this period as holily as possible, to be truly attentive to the Holy Spirit.'

An Asian cardinal shares this view: 'The conclave is a liturgy', he says, comparing its spiritual preparation to that of a homily. 'You think you have everything under control, but sometimes it's a comma added at the last minute that touches a heart.'

Cardinal Jean-Paul Vesco OP, Archbishop of Algiers, spoke of a 'true time of spiritual discernment': 'We must discover the one whom the Lord has already chosen', he explained. During a Mass at St Peter's Basilica, Cardinal Baldassare Reina, Vicar of the Diocese of Rome, called on his fellow clergy to take a radical step: 'We must enter into God's dream entrusted to our poor hands.'

A Sunday Without a Pope

May 4 On this Sunday in the southern suburbs of Rome, Cardinal Christoph Schönborn OP has just celebrated Mass in his parish of the Divine Worker Jesus. The concrete church, built in the 1960s and 1970s, does not really have the charm of the ancient Roman basilicas, but it is filled with young families. This morning, three baptisms were celebrated by the former archbishop of Vienna. It is customary for cardinals preparing to enter conclave to celebrate Sunday Mass in their Roman parish, symbolising the fundamental link between the city and the papacy. 'The Roman parishes elect the bishop of Rome,' insisted the Austrian cardinal, who spoke in his homily of Peter's tomb and his martyrdom as "the glory of Rome".'

Relaxed, he confided with a smile that he had no chance of being elected pope because of his age: he had celebrated his 80th birthday in January of this year. He commented on the Gospel of the day, which was very timely: the famous passage from chapter 21 of St John's Gospel where Jesus asks Peter, 'Simon, son of John, do you love me? do you truly love me?' For the Austrian cardinal, some people might stop at human criteria when entering the conclave: 'The next pope should be someone "prudent", "sympathetic" or a good "organiser".' But for him, these qualities are not essential. 'Jesus asks only one thing: "Peter, do you love me?"' the preacher reminded us. 'That is the only thing that matters: everything else will follow.'

Pursuing the Investigation

By taking an oath, each cardinal pledges to keep the proceedings of the congregations secret. Some scrupulously respect this commitment, avoiding journalists. Others let a few words slip through, or even grant private interviews.

An African cardinal, who is very discreet in the media, insists on the importance of cutting oneself off from the world. 'This is not indifference. We carry the world in our prayers, but we must remain vigilant against attempts to influence us.'

Some cardinals received detailed booklets at the entrance to the Vatican containing profiles of the *papabili*, including their ideological affinities and positions. 'There's money behind this', a cardinal whispered to me, showing me one of these documents. Other attempts to influence the vote took the form of letters from the faithful sent to inside the Paul VI Hall, addressing issues such as abuse and synodality. Cardinal Blase Cupich, Archbishop of Chicago, met discreetly in a restaurant in central Rome with Juan Carlos Cruz, a Chilean victim who has become one of the faces of the fight against abuse in the Church.

One member of the conclave says he is not interested in outside pressure. 'I am guided by the programme of the congregations', he confides, explaining that he does not feel the need to investigate all the candidates in detail. Others, on the contrary, seek information in the press, on the Internet, or from trusted individuals, including journalists. One cardinal believes that there is a gap between what he reads in the media and what is happening inside the Vatican. 'I don't feel that there is a political campaign', he asserts.

What is the Profile for the Next Pope?

Francis' unique pontificate weighed heavily on this pre-conclave. Cardinal Albert Malcolm Ranjith, Archbishop of Colombo, said on Sunday the 4th of May that he hoped to elect a pontiff 'worthy and capable of being, in a sense, close to this great pope'. A 'consensus for continuity' seems to be emerging within the Sacred College, according to Salvadoran Gregorio Rosa Chavez, but also many other cardinals interviewed. All agree that the next pope, like Francis, must have a 'pastoral style'.

With Francis, the College of Cardinals has become the reflection of a Church that has shifted towards the South. An African cardinal elector emphasises, however, that Europe should not be sidelined. 'Europe is the mother of other Churches', he affirms. Cardinal Bustillo, for his part, calls for balance: 'We need both: the enthusiasm of the young Churches and the experience of Europe. I will not vote for a passport, a culture or a skin colour.'

Proficiency in Italian has been a subject of debate. For some, it is essential for the Bishop of Rome. Others believe that a pope can perfect his command of the language after his election. 'It's true that we would like a pope who speaks two or three languages', confided one of the 133 cardinal electors.

On the other hand, there seems to be a consensus on age: 'In the conclave, if you're under 60 or over 80, you're safe', jokes a young cardinal. An African cardinal notes that if the youngest member of the college, Cardinal Mykola Bychok of Australia, who is 45, were elected, he could remain pope for more than forty years!

Some, such as Cardinal Raphael Sako, already claim to have a name in mind. But for others, the choice remains to be made. An African cardinal concludes: 'I think I will decide in the Sistine Chapel, after a final prayer. In the meantime, I am leaving all doors open, because I don't want to miss the right one.' The time to vote is approaching. A 'Last Judgement'—in keeping with Michelangelo's eloquent fresco.

On the Eve of the Conclave

May 6. The temperature drops in Rome. The sky is cloudy. But beneath the red birettas of the 133 cardinals called to enter the conclave the following day, minds are racing. 'We are helpless', confides Cardinal Francesco Montenegro, Archbishop Emeritus of Agrigento, before entering the gates of the Holy Office. Like many, the 78-year-old Sicilian attests to the difficulty of the task ahead. More than eight out of ten voters have never participated in a conclave. And Pope Francis has rarely consulted the College of Cardinals during his pontificate, even though some members have been able to forge links during synods organised in Rome. Many admitted that they still did not know each other well, a feeling reinforced by the unprecedented geographical dispersion of the college. Seventy different countries. Some call to mind the ambience of the general congregations held in the amphitheatre of the Paul VI Hall.

Unlike the conclave, non-voting cardinals—those over the age of 80—may also attend the Congregations and express their opinions. Although the atmosphere remains subdued, it can sometimes become heated, as was the case during a speech by Cardinal Joseph Zen, the 93-year-old bishop emeritus of Hong Kong and a fierce critic of certain aspects of Francis' pontificate. Cardinal Joseph Coutts, Archbishop Emeritus of Karachi, commented ironically on this occasion: 'The arguments haven't even begun.'

Over the past few days, the 133 electors have had to listen to, assimilate and digest more than 250 speeches by their peers, each lasting five minutes. 'We have tried to get a vision of the whole Church', explains Cardinal Anders Arborelius, 75, Bishop of Stockholm, who admits feeling somewhat tired in the face of such intensity.

While everyone can speak, not all contributions receive the same attention, confided an experienced European cardinal. Yet it is at this moment that the *papabili* are often identified: 'In 2013, when Bergoglio stood up and spoke, we pricked up our ears', he recalls.

The format of the congregations is disconcerting to some. 'It's the old world', says a European cardinal, accustomed to the more participatory recent synods. 'The speeches follow one another without an agenda. They are supposed to last five minutes, but some speak for a quarter of an hour', he adds, admitting that he has sometimes felt a little faint.

3.

At the Conclave, Peter Returns

The long-awaited day has dawned on Rome. It is now a matter of hours or days before we know the name of the 267th successor to Peter. On this morning of May 7, the press room at the top of Via della Conciliazione is packed to the rafters. It is difficult to find a free seat. Never has the saying been so true: all roads lead to Rome. Catholicism, with its universal claims, can verify that its garden still exists on a global scale. Secular or religious, the media have instinctively understood that the man in white whose name will soon be revealed is a protector for all humanity. A mere mortal, but one who protects us from the most destructive forces of our century. It seems that the promise made to the humble fisherman of Galilee is now being fulfilled, in the midst of the cacophony of nations: 'And I say to you: You are Peter, and on this rock I will build my Church; and the power of Death shall not prevail against it' (Mt 16:18).

Clear skies, despite forecasts of sudden showers. In the area around St Peter's Square, secured by a large deployment of security forces, there were no large crowds for this first stage of the day's entry into conclave. However, many faithful, priests and representatives of numerous religious orders—as well as a few tourists—gathered in St Peter's Basilica as soon as it opened, to surround the cardinal electors and non-electors during these decisive hours. Among them was Sister Maria, a nun from the Philippines who lives in Rome, who said she wanted to 'accompany the cardinals in prayer' and was convinced that they would 'make the right choice'. 'We have experienced the sadness of Pope Francis' death, we will now be able to rejoice in the election of his successor', said Thomas, an American Catholic who came from Maryland with his wife and four children. 'Tonight, we will come back to see the smoke, which will be white, I hope', he said, excited to experience a 'historic moment' up close.

The Holy Spirit Called Upon for Help

It is 10 am. Start of the Mass *pro eligendo romano pontifice.* All cardinals—electors or not—pray in St Peter's Basilica, this time 'for the election of the Roman Pontiff'. Bishops, priests, deacons, religious and lay faithful present in Rome may also participate in the celebration, thus manifesting communion in prayer of the whole Church at such an important moment. Everything is provided for in the *Ordo rituum conclavis.*

Broadcast by Vatican media, the Mass is presided over by the dean of the Sacred College, Italian Cardinal Giovanni Battista Re. At 91, he presided over the general congregations, the closed-door meetings during which the cardinals take stock of the pontificate of Francis. The former prefect of the Congregation for Bishops, who also presided over the funeral Mass of Pope Francis, will not be able to participate in the conclave as he is over 80 years old. A key figure during the *sede vacante* (vacant seat) period, he now sees the conclave slipping away from him. This afternoon, he will remain outside the Sistine Chapel, leaving his role as President to another Italian, Cardinal Pietro Parolin, the most senior cardinal in the order of bishops.

Cardinal Re's Final Recommendations

From his pulpit, aware that history would remember his words, Cardinal Re began by bringing the audience back to reality. No one should forget the gravity of the moment for the Church. The transition from one pope to another is never a foregone conclusion. 'We are here to invoke the help of the Holy Spirit, to implore his light and strength, so that the pope whom the Church and humanity need at this difficult, complex and troubled turning point in history may be elected.'

Cardinal Re emphasises the role of the next pope in steer the ship of St Peter's despite the international turmoil: 'Today's world expects much from the Church in safeguarding these fundamental human and spiritual values, without which human coexistence cannot improve or bring good to future generations.'

He then addresses the consciences of the cardinals directly:

> 'Praying, invoking the Holy Spirit, is the only proper attitude to take as the cardinal electors prepare for an act of the highest human and ecclesial responsibility and a choice of exceptional importance; a human act for which all personal considerations must be set aside, having only the God of Jesus Christ and the good of the Church and of humanity in mind and in heart.'

This reminder is not unnecessary, given that rumours and *bombes puzzolenti* ('stink bombs', one might say) have weighed heavily on the atmosphere in recent days. Not all cardinals are angels, and some are pushing their pawns or their agenda, even if it means upsetting others.

Misinformation and Rumour

None of the *papabili* escape these targeted attacks. The higher they rise, the stronger the wind blows. A few days earlier, Emmanuel Macron had been accused by the Italian press of wanting to influence the election of the next pontiff. Furthermore, according to the Milanese newspaper *La Verità*, the French president himself 'wants to choose the pope'. 'Macron's hubris knows no bounds', denounced *Il Tempo*. As the conclave approached, the head of state was accused of stepping up his efforts to impose the Archbishop of Marseille, Jean-Marc Aveline. He was 'entrenched' trumpeted the conservative daily *Libero*. At issue was a lunch in Rome. Five days after the death of Pope Francis, Emmanuel Macron had gathered four French cardinals for lunch at the French embassy in the Eternal City: Jean-Marc Aveline, *papabili*, Christophe Pierre, Apostolic Nuncio to the United States, Philippe Barbarin, Archbishop Emeritus of Lyon, and François Bustillo, Bishop of Ajaccio.

According to *Il Tempo*, the incumbent president in Élysée had questioned them about how to build consensus around his favourite candidate.

In *Le Figaro*, Guillaume Tabard deflated the balloon: 'A close examination of the chronology shows how the rumour spread through conflations and a lack of verified information. Cardinal Erdö [Archbishop of Budapest] reported contacts between Emmanuel Macron and the five French cardinals to block Cardinal Sarah's path.' This is what was mentioned in a tweet by someone named

Stornsen, written on April 22 at 11:41 am, twenty-four hours after the announcement of Francis' death. The date of the funeral had not yet been set and the lunch at the Villa Bonaparte was not yet scheduled. When questioned by *Le Figaro*, the President of the Republic, Cardinal Erdö and the French cardinals who attended the lunch, all formally denied this allegation and even any consideration of any hoped-for outcome. 'Emmanuel Macron assured us that he had had absolutely no contact with French voters prior to this lunch on 26 April.'

We are far from the lofty perspective of the cardinals who are about to lock themselves in the Sistine Chapel. Cardinal Re continued his homily by quoting the apostolic constitution *Universi Dominici gregis*, which governs the details of the conclave: 'Everything contributes to nourishing the awareness of the presence of God, before whom each one will one day have to appear to be judged.' Cardinal Re recalled the fundamental quality of a pope, namely 'love to the point of total self-giving'. He added, regarding the Petrine charism: 'Among the tasks of each successor of Peter is that of fostering communion: communion of all Christians with Christ; communion of the bishops with the pope; communion of the bishops among themselves.'

Peter, Still Alive

Aware of the weight of rumours and misinformation, Cardinal Re also emphasised the need to overcome divisions: 'There is a strong call to maintain the unity of the Church in the path laid out by Christ to the apostles. The unity of the Church is willed by Christ; a unity that does not mean uniformity, but a solid and profound communion and profound communion in diversity, provided that we remain fully faithful to the Gospel.' He concluded by paying tribute to the vision of contemporary popes: 'Let us pray that the Holy Spirit, who has given us a series of truly holy and great pontiffs over the last hundred years, will give us a new pope according to the heart of God, for the good of the Church and of humanity.' The closing words, in the form of a supplication, are noteworthy: 'Let us pray that God will grant the Church a pope who will best awaken the consciences of all and the moral and spiritual energies in today's society.'

Cardinal Re recalled that the successor of Peter is part of a very long unbroken tradition. His originality is combined with Tradition: 'Each pope continues to embody Peter and his mission and thus represents Christ on earth; he is the rock on which the Church is built. The election of the new pope is not a simple succession of persons, but it is always the apostle Peter who returns.'

Peter is coming back, certainly, but no one knows where he will come from. Vatican experts do not know and say they are ready for anything. The outcome of the conclave starting on May 7 was really up in the air. First, because the rules of this closed-door vote with no formal candidates make it hard for observers to understand all the codes and figure it out. Bound by secrecy since they entered the general congregations, the cardinals cannot discuss the trends and sensibilities within the College of Cardinals. And very often, they themselves do not have a clear idea of the scenario that will unfold beneath the frescoes of the Sistine Chapel.

The Accommodation of the Cardinals at Saint Martha's

In recent days, all the usual occupants of the two houses of Santa Marta—the old and the new—have had to leave the premises, which have been restructured and secured in order to accommodate the 133 cardinal electors. Their installation in the rooms of this Vatican residence began on May 6. Only suite 201—the apartment of the late pontiff—remains unoccupied. It remains sealed until the election of the new pope, who may take up residence there in the first days of his pontificate. He will also be invited to visit the pontifical apartments of the Apostolic Palace, which were also sealed after the death of Francis on April 21 and may choose to move in there.

The Santa Marta house was inaugurated by John Paul II in 1996. It was originally designed for a conclave. The cardinals who participated in the two conclaves of 1978—including Joseph Ratzinger, the future Benedict XVI—were then housed on camp beds in the corridors of the Apostolic Palace, in very spartan and difficult conditions in the heat of the Roman summer. With an investment of US $20 million, John Paul II therefore decided to support the construction of a new, more modern and secure building for the conclave dedicated to electing his successor.

This building, which has 129 rooms, is usually used as a guest house, but some priests working at the Roman Curia live there full-time, except during a conclave. To everyone's surprise, after his election in 2013, Pope Francis chose to reside there permanently, taking possession of the suite occupied by Patriarch Bartholomew of Constantinople, who had come to the Vatican for his installation Mass.

An Extraordinary Ritual

Once the cardinals are settled and cut off from the world, without mobile phones or any other means of communication, what will they do? As Jean-Marie Guénois writes so aptly in *Le Figaro*:

> 'the conclave's agenda is set in advance. Its solid legal framework, the "apostolic constitution", lays down the procedures in detail, from the death of the pope and his funeral to the election of his successor. In terms of procedure, therefore, the conclave's programme holds no surprises. As for the music that will actually be played, that is another matter: it depends on the conductor, the Holy Spirit, according to Catholic doctrine, and his musicians, the cardinals. This conclave "behind the scenes" is full of secret chords and arpegios.'

A few steps from St Peter's Square, on 7 May, the cardinals prepared to vote after hearing the sermon of Cardinal Cantalamessa. The last exhortation before the leap into the unknown. Could Peter's successor be elected tonight? In truth, no pope has ever been elected in the first round. This cannot be conclusive, explains an experienced colleague, because it is intended as a 'primary' election, to show the cardinals who the first three or four elected are and how many votes they have received. It is on the basis of this real poll that the dynamics of the papal election will unfold.

The Sistine Chapel, a Spiritual Gem

The Sistine Chapel, usually part of the tourist circuit of the Vatican Museums, has once again become a sacred place for a few days, reviving the tradition of the conclaves that have been held there since the election of Pope Alexander VI Borgia in 1492. It was designed as a living catechesis that bears witness to the relationship between humanity and the infinite. This highly ambitious project of the 15th century led to the construction of a rectangular building over 40 metres long and 13 metres high. The frescoes, commissioned by Pope Sixtus IV, were painted between 1481 and 1483 by artists from the

Florentine School. Why are they so striking? Because, according to experts, they constitute a visual narrative celebrating the history of salvation, intertwining events from the Old Testament, with panels depicting the life of Moses, and those from the New Testament, with frescoes focusing on the life of Christ. In short, a veritable Bible in pictures. It must have had an even more impressive impact on visitors of the past, who were not bombarded by digital images as we are today.

At a moment when time stands still in the press room and all around the Vatican, it is worth taking a look back at this centuries-old history. Although the Sistine Chapel has traditionally been the venue for many conclaves, with an interruption in the 16th century, it was in Venice that the cardinals elected Pope Pius VII after the tragic death of his predecessor Pius VI, who had been deported by revolutionary France. His successors Leo XIII, Pius VIII, Gregory XVI and Pius IX were elected at the Quirinal Palace, now occupied by the Presidency of the Italian Republic. The tradition of the conclave in the Sistine Chapel was restored in 1878 for the election of Pope Leo XIII, eight years after the fall of the Papal States, in a context of rupture with Italy, the pope considering himself a 'prisoner' in the Vatican. But it was not until 1996 that Pope John Paul II formally established the Sistine Chapel as the official venue for conclaves. It was a fruitful idea that has captured the imagination of the entire world.

Meeting in the Pauline Chapel

The 133 cardinal electors will first meet at 4:15 pm in the Pauline Chapel of the Apostolic Palace in the Vatican for a short prayer introducing the procession to the Sistine Chapel. In this Pauline Chapel, which is not usually open to visitors, there two frescoes by Michelangelo illustrate the martyrdom of Saint Peter and the conversion of Saint Paul. The cardinals will be able to gaze into the mysterious eyes of Saint Peter, crucified upside down, who seems to be warning the viewer who is observing him. This election is a serious matter which involves the life of the Church. The Pauline Chapel, renovated in 2009, is separated from the Sistine Chapel by the splendid *Sala Regia*, the hall of honour of the Apostolic Palace. The images broadcast live by the Vatican are magnificent.

We do not yet know which names the cardinals will write on the rectangular ballots in a few moments. However, it is easy to imagine the atmosphere. For the occasion, the Sistine Chapel has been furnished with cherry wood chairs marked with the name and first name of each cardinal elector, and tables covered beige fabric and burgundy satin, arranged in two rows at different levels. In front of the altar, under the 'Last Judgement', is a table for the urn made of where the ballots will be deposited. On a lectern is the Gospel on which the cardinals take their oath.

The Ballet of the Men in Red

At 4:22 pm in the press room, two large screens show images of the Sistine Chapel and men in red. We see the empty seats of those who, in a few moments, will slip in their first ballot. Serious, silent images, where the voters remain frozen in a kind of eternity in the Pauline Chapel. The ceremony is well-rehearsed and all they have to do is let themselves be carried along. Outside the chapel stand an impressive row of Swiss Guards and a few clergymen in immaculate surplices. The procession leaving the Pauline Chapel is led by the cross flanked by two candlesticks. Behind come the cantors and prelates, among whom are the secretary of the College of Cardinals, the master of liturgical celebrations and the cardinal responsible for the meditation.

The cardinals come next, divided according to the three orders that make up the College of Cardinals: first the deacons, then the priests, and finally the bishops. All will sing the long litany of the saints in Latin.

The magnificent images produced by the Vatican are even more beautiful than those in the film 'Conclave'. The faithful, gathered in the square, have their eyes fixed on the big screens. Reality is definitely stronger than fiction and there is an extraordinary sense of gravity in the air. Red hats and more red hats, like ripe fruit. But we must remember that the red here is the colour of blood shed, of loyalty to the point of giving one's own life. The cameras linger on an urn that resembles a flying saucer with two small golden horses seeming to gallop around it. The cardinals, meanwhile, stand motionless.

From One Chapel to Another

At 4:28 pm a drone offers a bird's-eye view of the entrance to the Pauline Chapel. The cardinals rise. For the procession into the Sistine Chapel, protocol dictates an order by rank and creation, from the most recent cardinal-deacon (Koovakad) to the oldest cardinal-bishop (Parolin). It is the latter who presides over the ceremony in a slow voice. The prayer alludes to the inner dispositions appropriate at this fateful hour. The procession begins to the rhythm of the litany of the saints: *Sancta Trinitas, miserere nobis! Sancta Maria, ora pro nobis*! The cross moves forward, majestically, in a ritual superior to any Hollywood script. Two candle bearers accompany the cross, bearing their candles with solemnity. *Ora pro nobis*. They now invoke Saint Joseph and the holy patriarchs. It is an understatement to say that this liturgy gives extraordinary weight to the upcoming vote.

The line of cardinals moves forward, calm as a scarlet river. They walk two by two, looking at their little white booklets. Saint Luke, Saint Mary Magdalene, all the saints are summoned as on Easter night. The first cardinals finally enter the Sistine Chapel. All their faces are seized by the solemnity of the moment. It is difficult to recognise them, so united are they. The Body of Christ. *Ecclesia*.

They bow before the altar, two by two. Among the four cardinal bishops who step forward first, the as yet little-known figure of Cardinal Prevost can be seen. Cardinal Aveline can be glimpsed briefly. Saint Boniface, Saint Callistus and Saint Thomas are called to the rescue. Cardinal Pizzaballa also bows before the altar. 'All you holy martyrs, pray for us; all you holy apostles pray for us.' Purple, red and black combine in an unchanging ballet. Stendhal had already written about this imaginary scene in his *Promenades dans Rome*. Above the cardinals is the famous fresco of the 'Last Judgement'. From 1536 to 1541, Michelangelo, much older, devoted four hundred and fifty-six days of work to it. A breathtaking masterpiece. When he discovered this fresco on the eve of All Saints' Day 1541, Pope Paul III is said to have broken down in tears, kneeling in prayer. It is easy to understand why.

At 4:43 pm, the procession is over. But the pleas continue: 'Saint Elizabeth, and all the saints pray for us. From all evil, deliver us, O Lord.' Cardinal Parolin remains standing in the middle of the Sistine Chapel. Cardinal Tagle can be seen looking very focused. Then Cardinal Aveline, whose eyes are almost closed. The whole Church is praying and the prayer of the world seems to fall back on the Sistine Chapel like an invisible and almost palpable rain. Cardinal Barbarin raises his eyes to Michelangelo's fresco. The hour is approaching.

At 4:50 pm, the cardinals remain standing during the litany. *Christe exaudi nos!* They all sing the *Veni Creator* together after laying down their birettas. Their faces resemble the Book of Revelation, parchment-like and tinted with the colours of all the continents. Cardinal Parolin is the first to pronounce the oath, which deserves to be quoted *in extenso*:

> We all, each and every one of us, cardinal electors present at this election of the Supreme Pontiff, promise, vow and swear to observe faithfully and scrupulously all the prescriptions contained in the apostolic constitution of the Supreme Pontiff John Paul II, *Universi Dominici gregis*, dated 22 February 1996. Likewise, we promise, vow and swear that whoever among us should, by divine disposition, be elected Roman Pontiff, will commit himself to exercise faithfully the *munus Petrinum* of pastor of the universal Church and will never cease to affirm and defend with courage the spiritual and temporal rights and the freedom of the Holy See. We promise and swear above all to keep with the utmost fidelity and with all, clerics and lay people, the secret of everything that in any way concerns the election of the Roman Pontiff and what takes place in the place of the election and which directly or indirectly concerns the ballots; not to violate this secrecy in any way either during or after the election of the new pontiff, unless explicit authorisation has been granted by the pope himself; not to assist or encourage any interference, opposition or any other form intervention by which secular authorities, of whatever order or degree, or any group or individuals might wish to interfere in the election of the Roman Pontiff.

Under Oath

A conclave is not without danger, and history has shown that the good of the Church is a fragile commodity. Each cardinal elector, according to the order of precedence, takes an oath in Latin using the following formula: 'And I, N. . ., Cardinal N, promise, vow and swear,' adding as he places his hand on the Gospel: 'So may God help me and these holy Gospels which I touch with my hand.'

First Cardinal Filoni, then Cardinal Tagle, Cardinal Sako, Cardinal Barbarin, Cardinal Turkson, Cardinal Sarah, Cardinal Burke, Cardinal Marx, etc. The 133 cardinals place their hands on the Gospel. When the last cardinal has taken the oath, the master of pontifical liturgical celebrations, Monsignor Diego Ravelli, pronounces the famous phrase *Extra omnes!* (All out!) so that those not participating in the conclave leave the Sistine Chapel. The Italian prelate then closes the heavy wooden door separating the chapel from the Sala Regia. It is 5:47 pm. The hour of the Spirit.

The Finger of God

Cardinal Prevost slept poorly. Too much pressure on his shoulders, no doubt. And then his name appeared, among those of others, as a possible successor to Francis . . . One cannot imagine becoming pope, one does not even dream of it. One would have to be mad, of course.

At that moment, the cardinal smiled as he recalled the shocking statement made a few days earlier by the Archbishop of Rabat, Cristóbal López Romero: 'If I am elected, I will flee to Sicily!'

And where could he go? In any case, this thought makes no sense. It won't be him. It would take an oversized ego to believe oneself capable of being the 267th successor of Peter. He is neither a superhero nor a megalomaniac. Now that he is locked up with all the other cardinal electors, he feels so close to Cardinal López Romero . . . He has no ambition either, he too is incapable of imagining himself in that role.

Cardinal Prevost was troubled by the fact that other cardinals, no doubt too kind, had thought of him. The first count of the votes was a shock. He did not even know whether to be honoured or frightened.

This day is not like any other. He senses it. Cardinal Prevost is finding it increasingly difficult to concentrate. He would so much like to surrender himself to silence and divine Providence.

But something in him resists. So many cardinals look peaceful in their beautiful red robes, listening to the Holy Spirit, the comforter. He too sang the *Veni Creator* with all his soul on 7 May in the Sistine Chapel. Why worry?

Charles Péguy's Advice

Although he was not a cardinal, Charles Péguy was an inspired author. And he was merciless with those men of God who lost sleep. 'I do not like those who do not sleep', says God. 'Sleep is a human person's friend. Sleep is God's friend. Sleep is perhaps my most beautiful creation. And I myself rested on the seventh day.' Cardinal Prevost knows his psalter well. Today, Psalm 130 comes to mind: 'Truly I have set my soul in silence and peace. Like a child on its mother's breast, even so is my soul.' Surrendering oneself to God is never easy, even when you have given your whole life to him. It is hard to live with, but that is how it is. Péguy adds, as a spiritual master: 'He who has a pure heart sleeps. And he who sleeps has a pure heart. That is the great secret of being tireless like a child.' Cardinal Prevost feels tired: exhausted, even. And yet, what a joy it is to be in the midst of all those cardinal electors who carry the Church and preside over its destiny! The destiny of the Church! What an honour, what an incalculable responsibility! The prelate groped his way forward, like one trying to find his way in the darkness.

A Name that Comes up Too Often

Today, his name has come up again. Cardinal Prevost is baffled by this movement he cannot control. Something strange, gentle and powerful, a deep force pushing him towards the light. He reassures himself by saying that other cardinals are far more qualified than him. The other names that are gaining votes are shields. His name? That of a poor mortal who was made a cardinal and is trying his best to live up to the position. It is becoming increasingly difficult to concentrate. Cardinal Prevost is not so much feverish as powerless. His thoughts wander in every direction and he is struggling to keep them in check. He knows that controlling one's thoughts is basic for the spiritual life. What is happening in this Sistine Chapel? Michelangelo's Christ, powerful and compelling, seems to be trying to tell him something. But what?

The American prelate is familiar with the naive stories of those popes who never believed they would become pope. There is the story of Saint Pius X who, with a return train ticket in his pocket, believed he had in his hands a safe-conduct to return home. Closer to home, Pope Francis knew exactly where his precious plane ticket to Buenos Aires was. He had even prepared his homily for Palm Sunday Mass. He hoped to be able to return in time to celebrate Holy Week in his diocese.

A Fall that Resembles Flight

Sitting like the others beneath Michelangelo's monumental fresco, Cardinal Prevost wondered what the outcome of the vote would be. Many of his colleagues had encouraged him discreetly. Too many, he thought. He wrote a name on his rectangular ballot paper, at the top of which was written: *Eligo in summum pontificem* (I elect as supreme pontiff). He took care to write legibly, in capital letters in the space below. The other voters did the same in applying themselves, looking thoughtful. Their writing must not be recognisable. Each cardinal takes turns going to the altar, holding his ballot paper—folded twice—in the air so that it is clearly visible, and pronounces the following oath in Latin: 'I take Christ the Lord, who will judge me, as my witness that I give my vote to the one whom, according to God, I judge should be elected.' Cardinal Prevost places his ballot on a tray and slides it into the ballot box in front of the scrutineers, bows towards the altar and returns to his place.

The Final Ballot

Now that all the ballots have been collected, a scrutineer shakes the ballot box to mix the ballots, transfers them to a second container and then to another, counts them . . . Two scrutineers write down the names, while a third reads them aloud, piercing the ballots with a needle through the word *Eligo* and connects them to each other. His name comes up again, louder than in the last ballot. How high will it go? Every time he hears his name spoken, Cardinal Prevost feels an invisible sword piercing his heart. He dares not meet the gaze of the others. He stares mechanically at the two stoves in the conclave room. The first is historic, dating from 1939, and is used to burn the ballots at the end of each vote. The second, installed in 2005, is used to burn smoke-producing chemicals, which give the smoke its colour: black or the—long-awaited—white. The American prelate knows that whoever reaches the threshold of eighty-nine votes will be elected. Emotion prevents him from counting, but his name keeps coming back to him. He should be rejoicing, exulting, but he feels as if the ground is giving way beneath his feet. He stares at the fresco of the 'Last Judgement' and those falling headfirst into the infernal abyss. He feels himself falling too, but not into hell. Into the arms of God, perhaps.

Accepto

As is the immemorial custom, Cardinal Prevost is asked whether he accepts or refuses the office of pope. Are they really talking to *him* at this moment? Everything is true, everything is simple, even if a little surreal. This solemn request, made before all the cardinals, is provided for in the apostolic constitution *Universi Dominici gregis*. John Paul II wished to ask 'the one who will be elected not to shirk the responsibility to which he is called, out of fear of its weight, but to humble himself to the plan of God's will.'

Cardinal Prevost changes his mind. He cannot back down. It is by the finger of God that he finds himself in this place. How can he turn back? 'For God, who imposes the burden on him, supports him with his hand so that the chosen one is not incapable of bearing it,' explains John Paul II. And he adds: 'God who gives this heavy burden is also the one who helps him to fulfil it, and the one who confers dignity, gives strength, so that the chosen one does not succumb under the weight of the mission.'

'Do you accept your canonical election as supreme pontiff?' Cardinal Prevost commits himself with a firm voice that surprises even himself. *Accepto*. Just as in the Gospel. He was elected. The master of pontifical liturgical ceremonies, acting as notary, with two ceremonial officers who are called upon at this time as witnesses, draws up a report of the acceptance of the new pope and the name he has taken.

Everything happens very quickly now. After the acceptance of the cardinal who has just revealed his name as pope, *Leo XIV*, the last ballots are burned to produce the famous white smoke. This signals the end of the conclave. Outside, crowds gather en masse in St Peter's Square. There were already so many people there the day before!

In the room known as the 'room of tears', the pope does not weep. Not yet. He is devastated and fulfilled at the same time. It is indescribable, a little like the distant day of his ordination to the priesthood. In this sacristy of the Sistine Chapel, he experiences the dizzying sensation of receiving the keys of Peter symbolically. Those keys open the impossible, those that bar the way to evil, those that keep the treasure of the deposit of faith inviolate. Leo XIV removes his cardinal's robes. Like the old man who becomes a new man through the effect of grace. He puts on the white cassock for the first time.

The Loggia, Balcony of the World

When the pope finally appears in the loggia, the applause does not stop. For Vatican experts, Cardinal Robert François Prevost is not really a surprise. He was on the list of '*papabili*'. The faithful do not know him yet, but they already love this Leo XIV, who is following in the footsteps of the great Leo XIII and his encyclical *Rerum novarum*.

At 7:25 pm Pope Leo XIV begins: 'Peace be with you all!' He repeats Jesus' greeting to his disciples locked in the Upper Room: 'In the evening, on the first day of the week, when the doors of the place where the disciples were gathered were locked for fear of the Jews, Jesus came and stood among them. He said to them, "Peace be with you!"' (Jn 20:19). Leo XIV repeated several times these words of his Lord: *Pace*. The peace of the risen Lord, not merely the absence of war, the fragile truce in Gaza or elsewhere, which can be called into question the very next day.

Pope Leo is trembling and emotional, and the square is moved to tears with him. Everything is new today, just like on Easter Sunday. In the crowd, people exchange biographical details about the new head of the Church. A former missionary bishop in Peru; a religious member of the Order of Saint Augustine, a member of the Curia, etc. It is all true, but not yet very detailed.

It is necessary here to quote extensively from the first words of Leo XIV: 'I would like this greeting of peace to enter your hearts, to reach your families, all people, wherever they may be, all peoples, the whole earth. Peace be with you all!' All ears are very attentive to the first words of the successor of Peter: 'This is the peace of the risen Christ, a disarmed and disarming peace, humble and persevering. It comes from God, who loves us all unconditionally.' He adds with restrained enthusiasm: 'God loves us, God loves you all, and evil will not triumph! We are all in God's hands. So, without fear, united hand in hand with God and with one another, let us move forward. We are disciples of Christ. Christ goes before us. The world needs his light.'

This statement is crucial because it has a certain programmatic quality. This was already true of his predecessors. In a few moments, Leo XIV outlined the path he intended to follow: 'I also wish to thank all the brother cardinals who have chosen me as Peter's successor, to walk with you, in a united Church, always seeking peace and justice, always working as men and women faithful to Jesus Christ, without fear, to proclaim the Gospel, to be missionaries.'

He ends with a deeply spiritual note. For the path he is taking is not merely humanistic or political. Leo XIV insists: 'I am a son of Saint Augustine, who said: "With you, I am a Christian; for you, I am a bishop." It is in this sense that we can all walk together towards the homeland that God has prepared for us.' The 'homeland', and not just patriotism; the city above, for it is true that Christians are citizens, as Saint Paul says.

American faithful, who have come for the occasion, flags of their homeland in their hands, leap for joy. At the moment of the traditional *urbi et orbi* blessing, young American girls look intently at the man in white. 'He's from Chicago!' exclaims Abigail with a touch of pride, accompanied by her student friends from Seattle. They are studying architecture at a university in Rome. Yanka says, beaming: 'I think from now on, Rome will be my second home!'

Abigail immediately replies, 'Leo XIV will bring peace back to the United States. It's so violent over there . . . We need a positive change. Religion and politics have been too closely intertwined for too long.' 'Yes, I agree', says the young man, 'but I don't think it will be easy'. Abigail has not yet been baptised. 'My parents decided to let me choose, but I went to a Catholic school . . .'

She looks up at the sky with an inspired look. 'It is strange, we've been able to see the whole cycle since Francis' funeral. There are so many signs for me . . . It is too many coincidences to be anything other than Providence.' Is not God the master of history and the papacy?

And that was the First Day

Today marks the first day of Pope Leo XIV's reign. It is still part of the conclave ritual. The new pope dines with the cardinals at the Santa Marta residence. Cardinal Vesco OP, Archbishop of Algiers, explained: 'It was very simple; he is a very simple. And that is very beautiful. The atmosphere was very joyful, very light-hearted, for everyone.' Cardinal Ladislav Nemet, Archbishop of Belgrade, who was seated next to the pope, recounted a joke made by the cardinals, who offered an 'explanation' on behalf of the pope: 'Until now, we had Francis, who spoke with wolves. Now we have a lion (*Leone* is a homonym for lion in Italian), who will chase away the wolves.' A vision, perhaps? Leo XIV, for his part, explained to his fellow cardinals the reason for his choice: 'We are in the midst of a new revolution. In the time of Leo XIII, it was the industrial revolution; now, we are in the midst of the digital revolution.' He then returned to his room to sleep.

It was on this occasion that Sister Nathalie Becquart was surprised to bump into him. She recounts: 'Cardinal Prevost lives in the Holy Office building, where I have lived since I arrived in Rome. He is my neighbour. It is not every day that you bump into a pope in your building, especially when you know him from before. We exchanged a few words in English. I congratulated him and told him that I would continue to pray for him and his new ministry. My superior general was also there, and we were able to share with him the joy and prayers of more than a thousand superior generals of women's religious congregations from around the world, who had gathered in Rome on the day of his election. Leo XIV was superior general of the Order of Saint Augustine. He knows what that means!'

She continues: 'I found him smiling, as calm as ever. He greeted those who were present and gave blessings. He is a very humble man, very discreet, balanced and serious. When he moved to the Palazzo two months ago, I saw him arrive one evening with his boxes. When we passed each other, we exchanged a few words very simply.'

Nothing has changed since he became pope, and it is the sleep of the just that Peter's successor has fallen into, after these few exchanges with his neighbours. He said yes. Now everything is in God's hands.

May 9. As the sun rises over Rome, the streets begin to fill with streams of pilgrims; churches open their doors and the first Masses are celebrated in thanksgiving. This is the case at the Basilica of Sant' Agostino, where Brother Cristiano, a young Augustinian friar wearing the black habit of his order, is standing. He has a big smile on his face despite his tired features: he has had little sleep. He is one of seven members of his community who reside in this important place of their order, since it is the site of the tomb of Saint Monica, mother of Saint Augustine. It is a place where Pope Francis liked to come to pray, as evidenced today by a commemorative plaque.

'Cardinal Prevost often came here', says the religious man, who is originally from Puglia. He explains that he knows the new pope well, particularly because he was Prior General of the order (2001–2013) in Rome. 'A son of Saint Augustine, it's a surprise, a great joy! We had, of course, read his name in the lists of *papabili* in the newspapers, but it is still truly unexpected', says Brother Cristiano. He was touched by Leo XIV's choice to present himself as a 'son of Saint Augustine', although he insists that Leo XIV is now the 'Pope of all and Bishop of Rome'.

'But it's true that emphasising his origins and education touched our hearts; it's a sign for our Order', he explains. Moreover, Brother Cristiano immediately draws a parallel between Leo XIV's first speech in the loggia and St Augustine's *City of God*: the same concern for peace. Those who were waiting or hoping for an African pope have thus had their wishes fulfilled in a way: Saint Augustine, the great African bishop, has here a successor who will undoubtedly continue God's work. Did he not write: 'Providence has guided the story of humanity from Adam to the end of history, as if it were the history of a single individual passing gradually from childhood to old age.' It is difficult to say where Pope Leo XIV fits into the chronology of this holy story. But there is no doubt that he is leading his flock towards heavenly Jerusalem.

Brother Cristiano is also very pleased with the name chosen by Cardinal Prevost because it evokes the figure of Leo XIII. 'He was a pope who did a lot of good for the Augustinians and loved us very much,' he explains. The Order, founded in the 13th century, had indeed experienced a period of decline when, in 1881, the Italian pope decided to revive it, pushing for the reopening of a novitiate in Italy.

Leo XIII then created several Augustinian cardinals and opened the causes for beatification of several members. 'He was the pope who canonised Saint Rita', emphasises Brother Cristiano, referring to the 14th century Augustinian nun known for being implored in 'hopeless causes'. Brother Cristiano finally highlights how much Leo XIII was a 'Marian pope', devoted to the Virgin Mary, and rejoices at the new pontiff's decision to recite the *Ave Maria* with the crowd. He also sheds light on the reference made by the new pontiff to the *Supplication of Pompeii* during his first speech. This prayer, recited every 8 May in the Marian shrine at the foot of Mount Vesuvius, was composed in 1883 by Blessed Bartolo Longo—whom the new pope is expected to canonise soon—echoing the first encyclical that Leo XIII dedicated to the rosary, *Supremi apostolatus officium*—the first of his eleven encyclicals on this devotion.

'Above all, Leo XIII was the pope of the Church's social doctrine, and that too is a sign for today's world', he concluded. 'It is a heavy cross that he will have to bear: pray for him.'

The time for the Pope Leo's first Mass, which also marks the end of the conclave, is approaching. Several cardinals have already expressed their joy. French Cardinal Jean-Paul Vesco OP rejoices: 'We have a good pope; we have a very good pope! I am very, very happy, as is the entire College of Cardinals. There was immense unanimity and immense joy. He has the entire College of Cardinals behind him. Let us move forward!'

Regarding the qualities of Leo XIV, Cardinal Vesco shares his thoughts: 'He is a man with an absolutely colossal wealth of experience. He is a religious man who entered the Order of Saint Augustine at the age of 17. He grew up in a community life. He was elected Superior General twice. However, a superior no longer belongs to himself and goes go out to meet the whole world. Of course, he has a nationality, but his identity is other than national, especially being a religious.'

As for his name, he admits to being a little taken aback: 'Extremely surprised, yes! After the name "Francis", which had made such an impression, I thought that this would be less obvious, that it would be old-fashioned . . . And then I heard the faithful in St Peter's Square shouting: *Leone*! *Leone*! It was incredible!'

At 11:00 am, the cardinals, dressed in white, are gathered in the Sistine Chapel. Not only the 132 cardinal electors who elected him yesterday, but also the older cardinals. The mitres and chasubles, almost all identical, reinforce the strong impression of unity. The readings from the Votive Mass of Thanksgiving after the Election of the Sovereign Pontiff evoke the figure of Peter. Obviously. However, the readings of the Mass of the day are no less significant, as we can read: 'This man is my chosen instrument to bring my name before pagans and pagan kings and before the people of Israel; ·I myself will show him how much he himself must suffer for my name." (Acts 9:15–16). Accompanied by the organ, the Sistine Chapel Choir sings the entrance chant: *Quoniam Dominus Altissimus, terribilis rex magnus super omnem terram.* It is one of the oldest religious choirs in the world. It comprises twenty adult singers—countertenors, tenors and basses—as well as around thirty young boys—sopranos and contraltos.

The new pope celebrates the liturgy in Latin with the papal *ferula*—the cross—of Benedict XVI. The readings are read in English and Spanish, echoing the dual American and Peruvian nationality of Robert Francis Prevost.

The Gospel, proclaimed in Italian, is taken from the text of St Matthew, in which Jesus says: 'You are Peter, and on this rock I will build my Church' (Mt 16:18). The new pope spoke briefly in English at the beginning of his homily, inviting the cardinals to 'recognise the wonders that God has done'.

Continuing in Italian, he recalled that through the figure of Jesus, 'God, in order to draw close and become accessible to human beings, revealed himself to us in the trusting eyes of a child, in the alert mind of a youth, in the mature features of an adult'.

Jesus thus shows 'a model of holy humanity that we can all imitate, with the promise of an eternal destiny that transcends all our limitations and capabilities', he emphasises.

In his response to Christ's question, Peter sees two aspects: 'the gift of God and the path to be followed in order to allow oneself to be transformed, dimensions inseparable from salvation, entrusted to the Church so that she may proclaim them for the good of the human race', explains Pope Leo XIV. 'God, in calling me by your vote to succeed the first of the apostles, entrusts this treasure to me so that, with his help, I may be its faithful administrator for the benefit of the entire mystical Body of the Church.' Using biblical metaphors, Leo XIV describes the Church as 'the city set on a hill, the ark of salvation sailing on the waves of history, a beacon that illuminates the nights of the world.' He specifies that the credibility of the Church is not expressed 'by the magnificence of its structures or the grandeur of its buildings—such as the edifice in which we find ourselves—but through the holiness of its members.'

Commenting on the attitude of the elites, Leo XIV evokes 'a world that considers Jesus to be a totally insignificant person, at best a curious character who can arouse wonder by his unusual way of speaking and acting'. But 'when his presence becomes inconvenient because of his demands for honesty and morality, this "world" will not hesitate to reject and eliminate him', he warns.

Another attitude is that of the people, who see Jesus as 'an upright man, courageous, who speaks well and says the right things, like other great prophets in the history of Israel. That is why they follow him, at least as long as they can do so without too much risk or inconvenience', he remarks. However, these people see Jesus as 'a man, and therefore, in times of danger, during the Passion, they abandon him and leave, disappointed', concludes the American-Peruvian pontiff.

'Even today, there are many contexts in which the Christian faith is considered absurd, reserved to weak and unintelligent people;

contexts where other certainties are preferred, such as technology, money, success, power, and pleasure', he notes.

The Pope emphasises that there are many environments 'in which believers are ridiculed, persecuted, despised or, at best, tolerated and pitied'. He also highlights 'the loss of the meaning of life, the forgetting of mercy, the violation of human dignity in its most dramatic forms, the crisis of the family and so many other wounds from which our society suffers considerably.'

He continues: 'There are contexts in which Jesus, although appreciated as a man, is reduced to a kind of charismatic leader or superman, and this is true not only among non-believers, but also among many baptised Christians who end up living, at this level, in a state of de facto atheism.' But, placing himself in the continuity with Pope Francis, he urges Christians to bear witness to their 'joyful faith in Jesus the Saviour', by also undertaking 'a daily journey of conversion': 'I say this first of all for myself, as the successor of Peter, as I begin my mission as bishop of the Church in Rome, called to preside over the universal Church in charity, according to the famous expression of Saint Ignatius of Antioch.' Leo XIV then quotes from Saint Ignatius' Letter to the Romans, in which the apostle Peter announces his impending death: 'Then I will truly be a disciple of Jesus Christ, when the world no longer sees my body.'

'These words refer more generally to an unconditional commitment for anyone who exercises authority in the Church: to disappear so that Christ may remain, to make oneself small so that he may be known and glorified, to devote oneself to the end so that no one misses the opportunity to know and love him', explained Leo XIV. 'May God grant me this grace, today and always, with the help of the tender intercession of Mary, Mother of the Church', concluded the new pontiff.

What strength, and yet what gentleness and tranquillity! The liturgy continues. The Universal Prayer is an opportunity to pray for unity, for the new pope, then for the bishops and missionaries, for priests, men and women religious, for the disappearance of resentment from the hearts of all, for those who are going through trials, for God to inspire young people with good projects, and for the elderly to be strengthened by the power of witness.

The Mass ends in solemn contemplation under the gaze of angels, Michelangelo's figures and the Swiss Guards. As he leaves the Sistine Chapel, Leo XIV is applauded by the cardinals and gives his blessing.

It is difficult to come back down to earth after this moment of grace. However, the mission awaits the new pope, and he enters his pontificate with confidence. St Peter's Square is teeming with pilgrims, as always. The jubilee crosses arrive with their bearers, supported by the chants and prayers of the faithful who are about to pass through the Holy Door. Pope Francis has opened the jubilee year; it will fall to Pope Leo to close it.

In the press room, journalists continue their interviews and write their articles. This is where Romilda Ferrauto, consultant to the director of the Holy See press office, is standing. For her, the name chosen by the pope is rather like a new birth. It has a very strong impact. While continuing in the footsteps of Pope Francis, Leo XIV is making his mark his own personality right from the start. He is a unifying figure, but also innovative. This is evident in the way he presents himself and in his speeches.

Of course, one cannot help but think of Leo XIII, a man of prayer and government. 'In Italy, Leo XIII is highly regarded and appreciated. With Leo XIV, we are continuing in the same vein, not only with Pope Francis, but also with Benedict XVI, for whom the figure of St Augustine was essential.' Leo XIV's first speech announced a programme already mentioned in the general congregations: unity in the Church and not just concern for the world and its peripheries.

What is this peace that Leo XIV speaks of? 'It is the peace of Christ, given to the apostles on the day after the Resurrection, which allows us to move forward to build the City of God, dear to Saint Augustine.' The new pope, during his appearance in the loggia, dressed in the traditional red mozzetta, was truly himself, neither imitating Benedict XVI nor Francis. That is his genius: to be himself, in the simplicity and tradition of the Church. A cardinal for two years, Leo XIV has had time to learn the ropes of the Curia while remaining a pastor, a guiding thread that he will be able to unravel throughout his pontificate.

Among the new pope's close circle is a French nun, Mother Yvonne Reungoat, former superior general of the Daughters of Mary Auxiliatrix, commonly known as the Salesians of Don Bosco. As a member of the Dicastery for Bishops, she worked for three years with Cardinal Prevost, also a member and then prefect of this of the Roman Curia dedicated to the appointment of bishops.

She noticed his depth and his ability to listen. She says:

> 'I was very happy when he was elected! From his very first speech, he positioned himself in line with Pope Francis, consistent with his life so far. He brings both novelty and continuity, building on what Pope Francis has begun and going beyond that, too, with a different personality. I am certain that the Church will continue on the path begun with the Synod. I was also struck by the fact that the word "peace" came up repeatedly in his speech. This is a sign of the importance of peace in the world, but also within the Church.'

Mother Yvonne draws on her own experience to provide an understanding of that of the new pope:

> 'I don't know how this synthesis works within him, because that is his own business, but it has created in him an open personality that allows him to form bonds, while also maintaining a critical mind. It is impossible to be indifferent to the great injustices of the world when we are directly confronted with poverty. I also experienced this when I was a nun in Africa: faced with daily poverty, not only material, but also in terms of education, health and life itself, I wanted to cry out against global injustice. Leo XIV has lived through these situations, he carries within him this confrontation, this tension, which is a good tension when we are looking for ways to reduce injustice and increase solidarity. As pope, he will certainly have the opportunity to work on this!'

Mother Yvonne was called upon to work with Cardinal Prevost;

> she attests to his great calm in delicate situations: 'My collaboration with him was a positive experience. When we, the three women, joined the Dicastery in 2022, he was a member like us, and then he became Prefect a year later, in 2023. I can confirm his ability to listen, his respect for everyone's thoughts, his ability to explore issues in depth with a perspective of faith. He does not remain on the surface, he is a man of great spiritual depth. He is also a serene man. In the face of challenges, I have always seen him remain calm in order to discern the paths that could open up. This is an important point in his new responsibility: this man does not lose his calm in difficult situations.'

And with the reform of the Curia, difficulties are likely to arise. Leo XIV will be able to draw on his experience and character to deal with them.

The curtain falls on this first act. The rest is up to God and the docility of the Pope and the faithful to allow themselves to be moved by the breath of the Spirit.

4.

A Missionary in the Vatican

Formed in an era of Deindustrialisation

On 14 September 1955, the Feast of the Exaltation of the Holy Cross in the Catholic calendar, little Robert Prevost was born in Chicago, Illinois. The city had changed a great deal since Tintin's visit in the 1930s and had nothing in common with the terrifying days of Al Capone's Mafia.

1955 saw the start of the Montgomery bus boycott following the arrest of Rosa Parks. Racial segregation remained a burning issue in the United States. It was also the year that Democrat Richard Joseph Daley became Mayor of Chicago. He is credited with saving Chicago from the same economic decline as other industrial cities in the Rust Belt—the region in the north-east of the United States on the brink of economic ruin. In Chicago, Richard Joseph Daley did very well. He was able to build a number of gigantic projects, including O'Hare International Airport and the Sears Tower. Richard Michael Daley, his son, in turn became mayor of the city. An American-style dynasty which lasted until 2011.

Ten years after the end of the Second World War, the steel industry that had made Chicago so prosperous began to decline, sending many working-class families, particularly Catholics, into a downward spiral of unemployment and excessive debt. The Prevost family enjoyed a slightly higher standard of living. From the generation of the future pope's grandparents onwards, they belonged to the educated middle class, but they were very involved in the Catholic parish community in the northern United States, where working-class and wealthier families socialised more easily than in the rest of society.

The priests were true community leaders in an America where 'papists' were considered a minority that was not always easy to get along with. Kennedy's election had not yet changed attitudes. The parish priests and their vicars ran the schools, the leisure associations, a whole small society, supported by solid families like the Prevosts, who were aware of their role in the community. There were many priests at the family table, and young Robert Francis easily immersed himself in this spiritual and convivial atmosphere where the priest was an accessible figure of authority.

The country's consumer society was exploding. In July 1955, at the other end of the United States, Disneyland opened in California. It was the first park to be built by the Walt Disney Company, a powerful symbol of American cultural hegemony based on leisure, which was to be accompanied by a rapid de-Christianisation of lifestyles, even if references to God continued to be made everywhere.

What was happening in the countries of the South American continent, which were predominantly Catholic? The political regimes were for the most part authoritarian and highly polarised, whether to the right or the left. They were a major concern in the Cold War and therefore attracted the attention of the United States. The local churches were very divided and did not really cooperate with those in the north of the continent. In the summer of 1955, the first General Conference of the Latin American and Caribbean Episcopate was held in Rio de Janeiro, Brazil. It was called for by Pope Pius XII and led to the creation of the Latin American Episcopal Conference (CELAM). It was the beginning of a long story that would one day take Robert Prevost all the way to Peru.

In the 1950s, the American dream hung on. But young Robert was growing up in a rapidly changing world: political instability, the Cold War, excessive consumerism . . . The Catholic Church, a minority in American society, was trying to carve out a place for itself in a cultural universe where points of reference were changing very rapidly.

A Name from France

The parents of the future Leo XIV, Louis Marius Prevost and Mildred Agnes Martínez, were both originally from Chicago. The family name Prevost, also spelt 'Prévost', is very common in France, but also in Quebec. It derives from the name of a former administrative function in France. In fact, in the Middle Ages, the *prévôt*, from the Latin *praepositus* (literally 'the pre-placed'), was a judicial officer or an ecclesiastical dignitary. In short, a predestined name for the man who would one day become the head of the Catholic Church.

His father, Louis Marius, was a school headmaster who had served as a lieutenant in the US Navy during the Mediterranean campaign in the Second World War. He was of French and Italian descent. This last point may seem like a wink of Providence. Indeed, there is often a link between popes and Italy, even when it seems invisible at first sight. The paternal grandfather of Argentine Pope Francis, Giovanni Angelo Bergoglio, was originally from Portacomaro Stazione, a hamlet in the municipality of Asti in Piedmont.

Louis Marius Prevost played a central role in the human and spiritual formation of his son, the future pope. He is described as a warm-hearted man, open to dialogue and imbued with the Catholic faith. Unlike many men in the 1950s, he did not believe that passing on the faith to children was a task for women alone. For a long time, he worked as a catechist in his parish.

Louis Marius and his Spanish-born wife, Mildred Martínez, brought up their three sons—Louis Martín, John Joseph and Robert Francis—in an environment where cultural traditions intersected. Mildred, renowned for her cuisine blending Spanish and Italian flavours, embodies the art of entertaining friends, priests and sometimes even bishops. The couple passed on the fundamental values of the Gospel to their children. The two brothers of Leo XIV remained attached to the Christian faith throughout their lives. Indeed John made a career in Catholic teaching.

African Blood in their Veins

Mildred Agnes Prevost was a librarian, who was very involved in the life of their parish. She was the epitome of the American melting pot. Mildred Agnes was of diverse ancestry: Louisiana Creole, Haitian, French and Spanish. Her father, Joseph Martínez—a native of Haiti—and her mother Louise Baquiet—a mixed-race Creole from New Orleans—both came from mulatto families with black slave ancestors from Louisiana. Robert Prevost would become the only pope with sub-Saharan African ancestry, and the first pope with African ancestry, since the 5th century, notes the daily *La Croix*.

Little Robert's family tree was as vast as the world itself. His paternal grandmother, Suzanne Louise Marie Fontaine, was born on 2 February 1894 in Le Havre, Normandy. She moved to New York in 1915 after crossing the Atlantic on the boat *La Touraine*.

A product of this family of travellers, Robert spoke perfect English, Spanish and Italian. Today he also speaks French, although not fluently, and Portuguese. He can also read German and Latin without difficulty.

An Uneventful Family Life

Robert grew up in Dolton, a small town on the southern outskirts of Chicago, with his two brothers, Louis Martín and John Joseph. It was a fervent Catholic family, rooted in prayer, and a potential cradle of religious and priestly vocations. The parish of St Mary of the Assumption in Dolton now holds a real treasure. It is a photo from 1982 showing Pope John Paul II greeting a newly ordained young priest by the name of . . . Robert Francis Prevost. They say happiness has no history. And that seems to be true in the Prevost family. Little is known about his happy childhood and adolescence with his brothers and parents. But we can easily conjecture that this family life was the soil in which his human and Christian roots were able to develop.

Confidences of his Brother

Interviewed the day after the election of Leo XIV, his brother John Joseph obviously made no secret of his emotion. He took the opportunity to lift the veil on his brother, now Pope Leo XIV. He spoke about their trouble-free childhood: There aren't many people who can say: 'My brother is Pope!' He, John Prevost, can. 'To be honest, I hasn't been a chance to think about it" he confided, still digesting the news. "I don't think it's really sunk in yet. It's quite unreal". The Illinoisan learned the news like everyone else: 'I was reading when I got a message saying there was white smoke [at the Vatican], so I turned on the television. My niece said, "Look, the curtains are moving." We heard the name, and she screamed and I said, "O my gosh, here we go!"".

Until the opening of the conclave on Wednesday 7 May 2025 in the Vatican, Robert Francis Prevost had never seriously imagined becoming Peter's successor. During a telephone conversation on the eve of the first vote by the cardinals, the future pope kept telling him: 'No, it's not possible', recounts his brother. 'He was pushing it away and hoped it wouldn't come true, but it did come true. Nothing is impossible for God.'

If John Prevost is to be believed, the throne of Saint Peter seemed to have been promised to his brother for a long time: 'When he was 6 years old, a neighbour from the neighbourhood who used to play with us told him he would become the first American pope.' A prophetess from Chicago whose name we have lost, but who had a lightning inspiration!

As for who Robert Prevost will be under the skullcap of Leo XIV, his brother has no doubts: 'He's a very ordinary man. He'll take care of the disadvantaged and the most destitute. He will look after the interests of those who are not heard of. I think he will follow the path laid out by Pope Francis.'

He adds that his brother always wanted to become a priest: 'He knew right away. I don't think he ever questioned it; he never thought about anything else.'

At that age, children play with toy cars or soldiers. John confided that his brother had a wider range of recreational activities than the others. He was a happy, playful child like most little boys.

With his brothers, he played cowboys and Indians. But Robert Prevost also liked to 'play priest'. 'The ironing board was the altar', says his brother John. And the eldest, Louis, confirms in an interview just after the election: 'He used to run after me to give me "communion"; I found it boring to play that.' Great things can begin silently in the shadow of a simple playroom . . .

From the age of five, Robert attended St Mary of the Assumption parish school in Dolton, where as an altar boy he learned about the liturgy. His childhood friends remember him as a kind and quiet boy, earning him the affectionate nickname 'Saint' from his classmates.

He also thrived on sport, playing tennis seriously and continuing to do so for as long as he could. As a fan, his favourite sport was baseball, which was particularly popular in Chicago—he confirmed after his election that he had always been a fan of his hometown's White Socks team. This portrait presents the image of a sensible American teenager, without dramas, growing up peacefully as he discerned his vocation.

Robert felt a call to give everything to God. Probably, Leo XIV will say more some day about the awakening of a solid vocation. Robert persevered during his secondary studies at the minor seminary of the Order of Saint Augustine until 1973. In 1977, he obtained a bachelor's degree in mathematics from Villanova University (near Philadelphia). So he was both a Christian and a Cartesian. His scientific mind did not deter him from joining the Augustinians on 1 September 1977, where he took his first vows the following year. He made his solemn profession on 29 August 1981.

The following year, he obtained a degree in theology from the Catholic Theological Union (CTU) in Chicago.

Drawn to the Augustinians

But who are these famous Augustinian friars? The Order of Saint Augustine (in Latin, *Ordo Fratrum Sancti Augustini*; abbreviated to OSA), founded in the 13th century, today has around 2,500 members, including eighteen hundred priests in close on 50 countries, mainly in South America, Asia, Africa but also in the United Kingdom, Europe, the USA and Australia. Formerly known as the 'Order of the Hermits of Saint Augustine', it is a mendicant order of pontifical right,[1] which has followed the Rule of Saint Augustine since its foundation.

Its origins are from the hermits of Tuscany seeking to assist the people of Tuscany with new pastoral endeavours. The Order has important connections with the growth of universities in Europe and in later centuries follows an important missionary dimension. The Augustinians are also responsible for the papal sacristy and for the official parish of the Vatican, Santa Anna. Two communities of Augustinians therefore live permanently in the Vatican. You can imagine the emotion of these men in their black habits, just after the election to the pontificate of one of their own brothers. In fact, it was the Prior of the sacristy who was called in just after the newly elected pontiff left the Sistine Chapel to help him put on his pontifical vestments for the first time.

Saint Augustine, a veritable giant among the Fathers of the Church, had a major influence on the medieval West and inspired many

1. Publishers Note: 'Pontifical right' refers to ecclesiastical institutions, like religious orders or societies, that have been formally established or approved by the Holy See (the papacy).

different religious families. His *Confessions*, written at the end of the 4th century, served as a model for many Christians and, beyond that, for many men of good will. 'Love and do what you will', St Augustine advises those seeking a perfect path.

Peru

The first Augustinian mission was established in Peru on 19 September 1551 by the Spanish, from the Philippines Province[2] under the name of the Blessed Virgin Mary of Grace. The same Province also started missions in Iquitos in the Amazonian basin in 1901. The American Augustinians from Chicago came in 1964 starting in the missions of Chulucanas, in northern Peru. The Italian Augustinians went to another region in Peru, Apurimac in south central Peru, close to the Department of Cusco and Arequipa, in 1968.

They decided to join the newly created prelature of Chuquibambilla near Cusco, erected by the then pope, Pope Paul VI. Initially, the Apostolic Administrator, Father Lorenzo Miccheli, of the Order of Saint Augustine, and the Vicar General, Father Ettore Salimbeni, settled in Chuquibambilla. They founded new parishes in Cotabambas and Antabamba.

Today, the prelature of Chuquibambilla has around thirty parishes and various women's religious communities (Augustinian Sisters of Divine Love, Daughters of the Crucifix, Franciscan Hospitaler Oblates, Missionaries of Jesus the Word and Victim). This is a very fruitful area for a missionary Church that places social action at the heart of its daily service. Works of solidarity have been developed in collaboration with the other provinces: orphanages and homes for young people from poor families (Cotabambas, Chuquibambilla, Tambobamba), dispensaries and training centres. This is the dynamic that carried the young Father Prevost far from the throes of Western secularisation, where the Catholic Church was facing a seemingly inevitable decline.

Meeting Francis

Peru, a country that is relatively small on the scale of Latin America but nevertheless twice the size of France, received a visit from Pope

2. Publishers Note: Not belonging to the country named the Philippines.

Francis in January 2018; this trip enabled the Holy Father to meet and identify Archbishop Prevost.

They had met prior to that when the then Jorge Mario Bergoglio was Archbishop of Buenos Aires, Argentina, and Father Robert Prevost was Prior General of the Augustinians[3] and on visitation to his friars in Argentina. They met again shortly after Pope Francis was elected as Pope, when he visited Sant'Anna dei Palafrenieri, the parish church of Vatican City, where the then Prior General of the Augustinians, Father Robert Prevost, was also present. It is understood that Pope Francis enjoyed meeting him again and asked if there was some way he could help the Prior General. The then Father Prevost informed him that he was finishing his second term as Prior General in five months, to which Pope Francis rejoined would he like him, Pope Francis, to open the next General Chapter of the Order? Father Prevost agreed and Pope Francis did say the Mass on the feast of St Augustine at the Chiesa Sant'Agostino in Rome on the 28th of August 2013.

At the School of the Great Augustine

Augustine's ideal of community was based on imitating the fraternity described in the Acts of the Apostles: the community of the early Church that was one heart and one soul, in the image of the one triune God, and where material and spiritual goods were shared in common.

Unity is a leitmotif of Saint Augustine's, in the school of the mystery of Pentecost: 'To have the Holy Spirit', he writes, 'is to be part of that Church which speaks in all languages, and not to be part of it is not to have the Holy Spirit. If indeed the Holy Spirit has deigned to reveal himself through this gift of tongues, it is to teach us that we are his temple when we live in union with this Church which speaks them all. "Be one body," says the apostle Saint Paul, "one body and one spirit"'. So, for the community of believers, the greatest treasure is none other than sharing God.

---

3. Publishers Note: Fr Prevost was elected Prior General of the Augustinians in 2001 and held the office for 2 consecutive terms until 2013. He had previously been Provincial of the Augustinian Province of Our Mother of Good Counsel in Chicago from 1999 until his election as Prior General in 2001.

Pope Leo's Augustinian vein is touching hearts today. For the path opened up by Saint Augustine in Africa, at a time when Roman culture was in decline, is as relevant today as ever.

Saint Augustine is a philosophical and spiritual landmark who is sometimes better known outside the Church than to the faithful themselves. We spoke to the writer and philosopher Éric-Emmanuel Schmitt, a man of faith who collaborated with the Vatican to write *The Challenge of Jerusalem* in 2023. For him, the charisma of Leo XIV, nurtured by Saint Augustine, only needs to be developed to embody Christianity:

> That's what John Paul II achieved, and what Francis also understood. They presented themselves not simply as representatives of the Church, but as living witnesses to the Gospel. Through their speeches, their gestures, even their inner light, they conveyed something of their faith.: an openness to others, a concern not for themselves, but for the peace of the world, for the salvation of souls. A great pope doesn't just embody an institution: he carries the heart of Christianity.

Following in the footsteps of Saint Augustine and his predecessors, Leo XIV is already being seen as an apostle of peace.

Embodying and Uniting

Embodying Christianity, but also knowing how to bring people together, this is also part of the Augustinian charism. Éric-Emmanuel Schmitt has this advice for the new Pope: 'Go forward, but bring people with you!' The writer adds:

> 'I think he has the background to do that. He already embodies a form of universality: the son of a French father and an Italian mother, an American citizen who has lived a large part of his life in Latin America. It's a transnational identity, and one that ties in with the universality of Christianity. He is a man of many cultures, many languages and many stories.'

Robert's story is a holy one. He loves the Augustinian ideal of *Christus Totus*, understanding Christ as the Body of Christ, both in the Head and in its members. Augustine based his teaching on the Pauline concept of the *Corpus Christi* found in Paul's First Letter to the Corinthians: 'Now you are the body of Christ and individually members of it.' The distinction between Christ and his members is that Christ is the Saviour and his members have been saved. This is the spirituality that drives Robert Prevost, and which he wanted to embrace in order to mature his vocation.

The Call of Peru

Robert Francis Prevost was ordained a priest in the Order of Saint Augustine in Rome on 19 June 1982. He was 26 years old at the time. An achievement, but above all a new beginning that would soon take him far from Rome. For the time being, he was preparing a degree in canon law at the Pontifical University of St Thomas Aquinas [the Angelicum], which he obtained in 1984.

It was at this time that a major turning point occurred. He, the man from North America, was sent as a missionary with the Augustinians in Peru. It was a far cry from Chicago and jazz. Chulucanas, in the province of Morropón, lies close to the foothills of the Andes, in the middle of the dry tropical forest valleys irrigated by the Rio Piura.

He thus followed in the footsteps of the first heroic missionaries who had proclaimed the Christian faith in Peru.

Father Robert Prevost trained for a long time before throwing himself into this far-flung mission, serving the poorest of the poor on the edge of the world, far outside his comfort zone. He sat in the school, so to speak, of José de Acosta, who wrote in the 16th century:

> Before going to Peru, I had spent nineteen years in the Society, devoted to the study and teaching of the humanities, metaphysics and scholastic theology. Seventeen of the next twenty-two years were spent in the Indies, mostly in Peru. It would be more reasonable to praise the immense trials I went through there, where all my time was devoted to preaching in the temples or in the squares: the peregrinations over very hard and dangerous roads were long and painful. My constant concern was to help the Indians by providing them with teachers, catechism books, confession manuals and sermons.

Father Robert Prevost was of the same mind. He wanted to live out the motto of his Order every day: *Anima una et cor unum in Deum.*

What is our value if not the value of freely given love? The rest is 'rubbish' (1 Cor 4:13), as Saint Paul says. Charity alone will remain.

Canon Law and Pastoral Itinerancy

Father Robert Prevost was soon spotted for his talents as an organiser and superior. The remote territories of Peru were still missionary areas where needs were great and talents were quickly employed.

He was sent to the territory of Chulucanas, in the foothills of the Andes. This was not yet a diocese, but a prelature, that is, a jurisdiction of the Church where there was not enough people or human resources to justify it being administered by a bishop. There were few parishes, and the people, who are mostly descendants of the Quechua peoples, are poor.

As Father Robert was well trained in canon law, he took on the role of chancellor. This was an essential administrative role. He was mainly responsible for managing, authenticating and preserving the Prelature's official documents. Thus, until 1986, he was a privileged collaborator of the prelate, Bishop Juan Conway McNabb, and participated in the government of the local Church, while at the same time having a varied pastoral activity that enabled him to learn the Quechua language. A confrere, Father Pablo Larrán, testifies that the young missionary Robert Prevost regularly visited rural areas on horseback and greeted the inhabitants in their native language.

He never gave up his intellectual research, however. The following year, he defended a thesis in canon law on the role of the prior in his Order. For him, canon law was a prudent, precise and humane approach to the fragile human condition. What strikes you about this young religious is his character, which is both rational and spiritual.

Father Robert Prevost spent three years in the shadow of the Andes. These were years rich in experience and reflection on the link between a life of prayer, social integration and help for the most disadvantaged.

Missionary Fruitfulness

In Peru, this mission was still in its infancy. Father Prevost came to contribute his talents to a work begun in the 1960s. It was a turbulent time for the dictatorship, with General Juan Velasco Alvarado seizing power. He embarked on a forced policy of nationalisation and land reform. The democratic governments that followed would find it very difficult to survive.

At the time Father Prevost arrived in Peru, the country, which was going through an endemic economic crisis, was under constant threat from the revolutionary guerrilla group *Shining Path*. This Maoist movement launched an armed insurrection in 1980, right in the middle of the presidential campaign. Its members carried out attacks and political assassinations, forcibly gathering recruits and even massacring civilians. According to Peru's Truth and Reconciliation Commission, around 70,000 people were killed between 1980 and 2000.

Augustinian religious established a presence in Peru in 1968. They decided to join the newly created prelature of Chuquibambilla, erected by Paul VI. Initially, the Apostolic Administrator, Father Lorenzo Miccheli, of the Order of Saint Augustine, and the Vicar General, Father Ettore Salimbeni, settled in Chuquibambilla. They founded new parishes in Cotabambas and Antabamba.

Today, the prelature has around thirty parishes and various women's religious communities (Augustines of the Divine Love, Daughters of the Crucifix, Franciscan Hospitaler Oblates, Missionaries of Jesus the Word and Victim). This is a very fruitful area for a missionary Church that places social action at the heart of its daily service. Works of solidarity have been developed in collaboration with the Italian provinces: orphanages and homes for young people from poor families (Cotabambas, Chuquibambilla, Tambobamba), dispensaries and training centres. This is the dynamic that carried the young Father Prevost far from the throes of Western secularisation, where the Catholic Church was facing a seemingly inevitable decline.

In Peru, the creation of a network of seminaries had encouraged the growth of local clergy and their integration into parishes founded and run by religious. In 1998, several groups of Augustinian missionaries and lay volunteers from Italy began collaborating with *Operazione Mato Grosso*, which was working in Totora Oropeza in educational activities and catechesis. In 2006, in Cuzco, the Lucia Vannucci Maiani polyclinic was inaugurated, the work of the *Apurimac ONLUS* association, which provided health care for the poor in the prelature of Chuquibambilla and the outskirts of Cuzco. Wasn't this the best way to put into practice the precept of Saint Augustine: 'Love God, you can find nothing more worthy of your love'?

This religious experience in Peru left a profound, indelible mark on Father Prevost. In fact, he would never stop coming back to these highlands where the faith continued to flourish.

The Obedience of Religious

In 1987, however, Fr Prevost was called back to the United States. He returned to Chicago as vocation promoter and director of missions for the Augustinian province. The climate of the Cold War was fading. A treaty on nuclear forces had just been signed between President Ronald Reagan and Mikhail Gorbachev.

Father Prevost would only set foot on his native soil for one short year, living, like all religious, in obedience and self-denial. He had already learned to say 'Yes'. A religious does not belong to himself; he is a member of a large family within which his place can change according to need. He certainly learned good leadership from his position as director, however briefly.

It was probably a great joy for him to return to Peru in 1988. He spent the next ten years directing the Augustinian seminary in Trujillo and teaching canon law at the diocesan seminary, where he was also prefect of studies. He was therefore trained as a jurist in a subject that governed the internal relations of members of the Church. He seemed to have the gift of ubiquity. He was also a judge on the regional ecclesiastical tribunal and a member of the College of Consultors in Trujillo, a body made up of priests who are consulted on specific issues or in the event of a vacancy in the episcopal see. He ran a quasi-parish on the poor outskirts of the city, of which he was the founder and first parish priest. He loved this work in the field, shepherding his sheep on a day-to-day basis.

Pre-Inca Civilisations

Trujillo is nicknamed the 'city of eternal spring' thanks to its privileged climate and warm atmosphere. Today it is the capital of the *Libertad* region. Here, Father Prevost is able to experience the underlying soil on which the Gospel was planted. The region, dotted with countless archaeological sites, was populated by two important pre-Inca civilisations, the *Mochica* and the *Chimú*. *Chan Chan* is the largest pre-Columbian citadel in America.

La Libertad is also famous for its various *huacas*: tombs and pyramidal palaces of the coastal civilisations. Who could be unmimpressed? Who hasn't read *Tintin and the Temple of the Sun* or watched *The Mysterious Cities of Gold*, dreaming of this ancient world and the people who discovered and explored it? For missionaries, the challenge is to find ways of 'inculturating' the faith, not by imposing Western models but by bringing salvation through Jesus Christ. This requires a slow process of discernment.

Peru, the land of the Incas and Machu Picchu, where few Amerindian descendants remain, has had to work on its history, which was marked by Spanish colonisation. The wounds are still raw and the Augustinian friars know it. They have lived with the indigenous populations and know that the Christian faith does not erase culture but brings out the best in it. In the Jesuit church in Cuzco, for example, we see Jesus dressed as an Inca sharing with his disciples, at the Last Supper, the traditional Peruvian dish: *cuy chactao*, a variety of guinea pig fried under a stone that acts as a lid.

An Intense Parish Life

In Peru, Father Prevost quickly found his feet. Jonathan Cruz, who was one of his altar boys, remembers him fondly: 'He was very close to us. My family and I looked after the parish house downstairs in 1990. It was there that the first Augustinian priests arrived, and it was also there that Father Robert, who was the first parish priest, did a great deal of work throughout the Montserrat region.'

His simplicity and discretion left their mark on those around him. Brother Ramiro Castillo, a member of the Augustinian order, says: 'He was a very simple, quiet person. At meetings, he was always silent, thinking long and hard before giving his opinion.'

How could one not be deeply affected by this missionary experience at the end of the world? You can guess that Father Prevost lived those years as a true son of Saint Augustine. In secret, he put into practice the advice of the great North African saint. But once again came the call of obedience: Back to the fold! In 1999, he was elected provincial, responsible for the Augustinians in his home region covering the American Midwest.

The Makings of a Leader

His brothers had long since spotted in him the makings of a leader. Father Prevost was soon elected Prior General of the Order of Saint Augustine in 2001, at the age of 46: an exceptionally young age to head a religious congregation with worldwide reach. His election in the space of twenty minutes was one of the fastest in the history of the Order. He would be re-elected for a second term.

His style of government was not too authoritarian within his Order: he knew how to work collegially, with advisory bodies. This was his way of living Augustine's spirituality, which is based on community life. Father Prevost inspired a great deal of confidence. We are not yet in the Sistine Chapel, but the process is very much the same. He had a skilful blend of charity and ability. These qualities were also noted by those who worked with him from 2013 to 2014, when Father Prevost became Director of Studies at Saint Augustine's Priory in Chicago, as well as First Councillor and Vicar Provincial.

According to Father Vincent Cabanac, a religious of the Augustinians of the Assumption, this experience at the head of a missionary congregation left an indelible mark on the future Pope. During his two terms in office, and on two occasions, he toured the communities of his Order in some fifty countries, an international experience that Pope Francis did not have when he was elected, and which led Father Prevost to become a polyglot.

As a missionary, he had the experience of being uprooted, of a life far from his country of origin, a dimension that his predecessor did not have either, whose journey took place mainly in Argentina. Here again, the mark of Augustinian spirituality was strongly felt, with its attachment to unity—more communitarian than that of the Jesuits. It is more concerned with a global view of the human person. Father Prevost knows how to situate himself in a place in a spirit of service, working with the Christians in his care.

Bishop of Chiclayo

On 3 November 2014, Pope Francis appointed him Apostolic Administrator of the Diocese of Chiclayo and Titular Bishop of Sufar. He was installed on 7 November 2014 and received episcopal consecration on 12 December from the Apostolic Nuncio to Peru, James Patrick Green. On 26 September 2015, he was appointed Bishop of Chiclayo. This diocese has long been entrusted to Augustinian religious, with bishops belonging to this religious Order. In the same year, he acquired Peruvian nationality under the Concordat between the Holy See and Peru, which obliges bishops in Peru to be Peruvian citizens.

Chiclayo is the main town in the Lambayeque region of northern Peru. It is nestled in the fertile valley of the Rio Chancay, near the coast of the Pacific Ocean, 500 km south of the Ecuadorian border and almost 800 km north of Peru's capital, Lima.

The town's coat of arms reveals its attachment to Catholicism. The coat of arms features a white cross on a blue background, as the city is dedicated to the Immaculate Conception of the Virgin Mary.

His years as bishop in Chiclayo were rich in encounters. Father Prevost is reputed to be very close to his faithful: 'The Pope is a Chiclayan, long live the Pope!' chanted dozens of faithful gathered in front of Chiclayo Cathedral on 8 May, the evening of his election. During his first speech at the Vatican, in Italian, the new pontiff paid tribute in Spanish to his 'beloved diocese of Chiclayo', paying homage to its 'faithful people'. 'It was really moving, we couldn't stop crying', recalls Lula Botey, an estate agency manager, who loved his 'marvellous homilies', during which he 'invoked charity and urged politicians to think of the common good'.

In the Peruvian city of 600,000 inhabitants, many remember a man who was 'good', 'humble' and 'close to the people'. 'He visited the most disadvantaged and supported young people', says Luis Cherco, 57. 'He carefully defended his opinions, despite his "angelic face"', says Jesus Leon Angeles, coordinator of a Catholic group. 'If he had to talk about a situation in Peru, whether it was corruption or a massacre or deaths, he would state his position in the middle of Mass.' The Pope 'is going to put Chiclayo in the spotlight of the whole world', rejoices Victor Becerra, a 23-year-old businessman, while Bernardo Victor Heredia David, an 81-year-old former drama teacher, still finds it hard to believe in the appointment of his former bishop as Pope. He is a 'very simple' man whose 'familiarity made you feel good, and who brought many people closer to God'.

A Bishop in the Political Chaos of Peru

Within the Peruvian Bishops' Conference, Bishop Prevost is Vice-President and member of the Permanent Council from 2018 to 2023, and President of the Commission for Education and Culture from 2019 to 2023.

The Peruvian bishops played an important role in ensuring institutional stability during the successive political crises that led to the overthrows of presidents Pedro Pablo Kuczynski in 2018, Martín Vizcarra and Manuel Merino in 2020, and Pedro Castillo in 2022. A few days before his fall and arrest, Castillo, a radical leftist, was received by the President of the Bishops' Conference and by Bishop

Prevost, in order to find a peaceful solution 'at this very difficult time in Peruvian democratic life', as the bishops, who had previously had difficult relations with his administration, pointed out at the time.

Bishop Prevost is therefore well acquainted with the political and social realities of South America. It should be pointed out that within the Latin American episcopate, there are very few US nationals. The Peruvian Bishops' Conference does, however, have another American: Bishop Arthur Colgan, a religious of the Order of the Holy Cross, who has been Auxiliary Bishop of Chosica since 2015.

Meeting Francis

Peru, a country that is relatively small on the scale of Latin America but nevertheless twice the size of France, received a visit from Pope Francis in January 2018; this trip enabled the Holy Father to meet and identify Archbishop Prevost.

At the same time, Archbishop Prevost demonstrated his ability to make decisions in a highly sensitive matter, as reported in the daily *La Croix*. As Vice-President of the Peruvian Bishops' Conference, he had a front-row seat to the scandal in *Sodalicio*, a powerful ultra-conservative movement accused of numerous abuses. He continued to follow the affair after his appointment to Rome, until Francis dissolved *Sodalicio* last January, one of the last decisions taken by the late Pope. He was involved in the dismissal of Bishop José Antonio Eguren, his former metropolitan archbishop of Piura, who was a member of *Sodalicio* and found guilty of complicity in the scandal. 'He did more than the average Latin American bishop', says Paola Ugaz, the journalist behind the investigation into *Sodalicio*.

Another decisive meeting with Francis took place in Rome on 13 September 2019. The day before his birthday, Archbishop Prevost was invited to attend the General Chapter of his Order. Once a religious, always a religious. Even as a bishop, Robert Prevost retained the soul of an Augustinian religious—and even the habit! He sat in the front row, fully attentive. It would be an understatement to say that he drank in the words of Pope Francis to his brothers on 13 September: 'In this chapter, you have set yourselves the task of facing up to the most important challenges of the day, in the light of the Word of God, the magisterium of the Church and the great father Augustine.' With foresight, Francis showed how this charism is at the service of the universal Church.

Can Francis have imagined that his successor would be an Augustinian religious? 'You Augustinians', continued Francis, 'have been called to bear witness to this warm, living, visible, contagious charity of the Church, through a community life that clearly manifests the presence of the Risen Lord and his Spirit. Unity in charity—as your Constitutions also explain so well—is a central point of Saint Augustine's experience and spirituality, and a foundation of all Augustinian life.'

While community is an absolutely vital concept in this age when individualism reigns supreme, it is not enough. Francis concludes by forcefully emphasising:

> Let every member of the community be turned, with his first 'holy intention' of each day, towards seeking God, or allowing himself to be sought by God. This 'direction' should be declared, confessed and witnessed to among you without false modesty. The search for God cannot be veiled by other aims, even if they are generous and apostolic. For this is your first apostolate. We are here—you should be able to say among yourselves every day—because we are walking towards God. And since God is Love, we walk towards him in love.

In 2021, Archbishop Prevost was received by Francis in private audience. The content of their discussions is not known, but the pope was not in the habit of talking about the weather in such circumstances. For the Bishop of Chiclayo, a new and decisive turning point was on the horizon. Did he sense it? We can imagine that Francis had now perfectly identified the many talents of this missionary bishop in Peru, and that he was waiting for the right moment to entrust him with a mission of trust. 'He arrived in Peru, in a country marked by divisions, where he knew how to make the right choices and maintain dialogue with everyone', sums up Cardinal Christophe Pierre, Apostolic Nuncio to the United States.

This rare ability to listen and reconcile was one of the hallmarks of the Bishop of Chiclayo. This is a key point, and it struck everyone who had the opportunity to work with him over the long term. 'He comes from the United States', Mother Yvonne Reungoat, a French nun and former Superior General of the Daughters of Mary Help of Christians, commonly known as the Salesians of Don Bosco, tells us, 'but he has lived immersed in the people of Peru, faced with serious political crises, poverty, the consequences of the North-South divide . . . He is truly committed to his people in Peru. So he can build bridges, facilitate dialogue between realities that are *a priori* opposed to each other, even if it's difficult.'

In Rome, at the Dicastery for Bishops, Robert Prevost's rise within the Roman Curia has been the subject of speculation for several years, as he became a member of the Dicastery for Clergy in July 2019 and of the Dicastery for Bishops in November 2020. These discreet appointments can sometimes be a first clue to taking on greater responsibilities in the Curia.

In the Vatican administration, the Dicastery for Bishops is one of the most strategic, as it coordinates the process of appointing bishops in the dioceses of the countries of 'ancient Christendom', mainly in the northern hemisphere. Every fortnight in Rome, its twenty-five members—who before Francis were exclusively bishops and cardinals—meet in congregation. They study the profiles of candidates to renew the bishops of four dioceses per session. Their dossiers have been carefully prepared by the "apostolic nuncios," the Pope's ambassadors around the world who are responsible for identifying the best candidates for the episcopate.

In the Palazzo dei Congregazioni, which offers an unrestricted view of St Peter's Square, the members of the dicastery dissect the investigations of the nuncios. When everyone agrees, the prefect of the dicastery takes the files under his arm to present them to the Pope. For each vacant diocese, the head of the Catholic Church has a choice of three names ranked in order of relevance. This is the famous *terna*. Robert Francis Prevost knows this selection process inside out. When he joined this powerful congregation, led at the time by Canadian cardinal Marc Ouellet, in 2020, he saw hundreds of profiles of potential bishops pass through his hands. The Augustinian religious has encountered many complex situations of bishops who have failed in their responsibilities, always facing them with the same calm and serenity.

When it came to replacing Cardinal Ouellet, then, after 13 years at the head of the Dicastery for Bishops, Pope Francis turned almost naturally to Bishop Robert Francis Prevost. Prevost was undoubtedly overcome by a feeling of vertigo. But he did not back down.

> 'I had been part of the Dicastery for several years, and when he told me that he was "thinking about this possibility",

I said to the Holy Father: "You know that I am very happy in Peru. If you decide to appoint me or leave me where I am, I'll be happy; but if you ask me to take on a new role in the Church, I'll accept"', he told his religious order's website in 2023. He confided that he was following his 'vow of obedience' as an Augustinian religious: 'I have always done what I have been asked to do, whether in the Order or in the Church.'

Once again, Robert Francis Prevost had to pack his suitcase. In January 2023, he left his diocese of Chiclayo 'with difficulty' and crossed the Atlantic to Rome. There would be no going back. He didn't know that yet. 'He is a man who has been asked for everything, who has experienced everything,' confided Cardinal Jean-Paul Vesco OP, Archbishop of Algiers, the day after the conclave. 'As a religious myself, I can see from Cardinal Prevost's background that he was the right soldier. He was asked to do some training, he was sent to Peru, then back to the United States, he was bishop in Peru and then also administrator of a diocese that was having problems. He was appointed to the Roman Curia to head the Dicastery for Bishops . . . Basically, everyone who speaks of him, wherever he has been, speaks well of him', he says, happy to be returning to Algeria with the certainty that the Catholic Church had given itself 'the right Pope', the one it needed.

At the Dicastery for Bishops, his style and experience hit the nail on the head. On the set of KTO, Cardinal Aveline testifies: 'What impressed me about him is that he is an even-tempered, peaceful man who listens a lot.' The Archbishop of Marseille, who has also been a member of the Bishops' Dicastery since 2022, noticed a difference in atmosphere when the American took over. 'He has allowed the word to get around even more. It takes longer . . . But we take more time. He listens humbly', he says. Does that make Robert Francis Prevost indecisive? The man from Marseilles retorts: 'He's also a man of decision. Once we've decided on something, he sticks to it!'

French Cardinal Christophe Pierre is no different. Apostolic Nuncio in Washington, he worked with Robert Francis Prevost after his arrival at the Dicastery for Bishops. 'His qualities were quickly recognised in the Curia', adds Christophe Pierre analysing that

> He is a very calm, very human man. You can sense that he has a great deal of experience, forged during his previous ministries. His great calm does not prevent him from being

> decisive and using his authority. There are sometimes delicate situations where a decision has to be made . . . Robert Prevost has never shied away from his responsibilities. Benevolence and high standards, kindness and lucidity. Qualities that, as Pope, he will have to exercise.

With his appointment as head of the bishops, Robert Francis Prevost was naturally elevated to the dignity of cardinal. The celebration took place on 30 September 2023 in Rome's St Peter's Square, which was decorated with flowers for the occasion. On that day, Pope Francis awarded the cardinal's biretta—the famous red hat—to twenty-one cardinals. The list drawn up by the Argentine Pope included some of the leading figures in the College of Cardinals, which was due to meet after the death of Pope Francis. The Latin Patriarch of Jerusalem, Pierbattista Pizzaballa, Cardinal Stephen Chow of Hong Kong and the Frenchman Christophe Pierre were all part of this promotion. But Archbishop Prevost was the first to receive the cardinal's ring and hat from Francis—not that he ever wanted to be first. It took less than a minute, but the former missionary to Peru was clearly very moved. Already.

Under the sun that floods St Peter's Square, Pope Francis then commented on the story of Pentecost, pausing at the mention of the 'Parthians, Medes and Elamites', a long list of peoples that he compares to the cardinals 'from every part of the world, from the most diverse nations'. In his homily, the Pope multiplied the formulas that he had a unique gift for. Be 'evangelised evangelisers, not functionaries', he told them. The Church 'does not live on rents, still less on an archaeological heritage, however precious and noble it may be', he insisted. 'Pentecost is not a thing of the past; it is a creative act that God continually renews.'

Member of the Synod on Synodality

A week after the consistory, the new Cardinal Prevost was expected to open the Synod on Synodality, the major project to be launched by the Pope in 2021 to make the Church more inclusive and less clerical. This was the major challenge set by Pope Francis to the members of this unprecedented Synod, since lay men and women would be included and would sit alongside cardinals and bishops.

Sister Nathalie Becquart, under-secretary of the Synod of Bishops, remembers: 'He was part of the working groups on the role of bishops and the appointment process and criteria. In Latin America, he was in a diocese with few priests, so he had experience of working with lay people and having women in positions of responsibility.' During the months of October 2023 and 2024, the cardinal, without doing violence to his nature, would gradually reveal himself in this assembly that journalists describe as very polarised between progressives and conservatives.

In front of the press, he did not hesitate to say that the process of selecting candidates for the episcopate should be more synodal, that is it should involve priests, religious and above all lay people more. In his view, the nuncios—who are responsible for this task—need to reach out to people and parish groups. Of course, for Cardinal Prevost, a bishop must be a leader. But he cannot simply be a company administrator, because the Church needs pastors who know their people. However, in an interview with the Vatican media in 2023, he said that he did not want the choice of bishops to be the result of a democratic or political process. In the same vein, at the beginning of 2024, he was one of the Curia bishops who blocked the German Synod's plan for a 'Synodal Council'—a structure designed to enable democratically appointed lay representatives to participate fully in the governance of the Catholic Church in Germany.

At the synod assembly in autumn 2024, Cardinal Prevost was one of the most visible figures. In particular, he emphasised the importance of joint training for bishops from dioceses in the northern hemisphere and those in so-called 'mission' dioceses, calling for better links between Rome and the local Churches and for the selection of new bishops to be broadened through consultation with the people of God.

On the evening of Leo XIV's election, in a room of the Synod secretariat, Sister Nathalie Becquart was not surprised by the rapid choice of the cardinal electors.

> I think his wealth of experience must have played a part. Being a religious missionary, Superior General for twelve years, and therefore having travelled all over the world, having been a bishop in Peru, Prefect of the Dicastery for Bishops, speaking English, Spanish, Italian and a little French . . . These are all qualities! As an Augustinian religious, he must also have at heart the dimension of unity and communion, two very important elements in the rule of Saint Augustine.

Less than two years after receiving the cardinal's purple on the square in front of St Peter's Square, he appeared on the balcony of the basilica.

'Immediately after his speech in the Loggia, I can tell you that the Pope began to work and to deal with the difficult dossiers on the backburner . . Until now, he had one big problem to deal with every day in the Dicastery for Bishops. Now there will be several, every day', Cardinal Pierre tells us, before adding: 'It's a heavy burden, but the role of grace is obvious.'

Leo is a lion. He has changed his name and his size and, like Peter, he is going to learn to walk on water. Two days after his election, before the cardinals who had entrusted him with the keys to God's holy Church, the former missionary who had become Peter's successor admitted his limitations and humbly appealed for help: 'You are, dear cardinals, the Pope's closest collaborators, and that is a great comfort to me in accepting a burden that is clearly beyond my strength.' But he is certain: 'Your presence reminds me that the Lord, who has entrusted me with this mission, does not leave me alone to shoulder the responsibility.'

The Major Challenges Facing Leo XIV

For Pope Leo XIV, the white smoke above the Sistine Chapel is a fire that will endure. Cardinal Robert Francis Prevost has burnt all his ships and he will never turn back. His friends and family, the faithful of his diocese of Chiclayo, priests and religious of all kinds: from now on, they will come to him. In Rome.

In the Eternal City, the elders still tell the story of the Pope who came from Poland with his small suitcase and left his slippers, ready for use, in his room in Krakow. Prudence, in the Christian system, always has its limits, warns Saint Paul: 'The wisdom of this world is foolishness in the sight of God' (1 Cor 3:19). Leaving his homeland was a wrench for Leo XIV. It was the same for Karol Wojtyła, nurtured in the Polish bosom from his earliest childhood: 'The Polish cardinal was faced with a challenge unknown to his predecessors: to find harmony between his nationality and the universal role of the pope', wrote Tadeusz Mazowiecki, the first Polish leader to succeed the Communist potentates. 'For a long time, popes had been Italian: in a way, they had no nationality. But he had to solve the problem of reconciling his deep national roots with the universal mission to which he had been called.'

It is a fact: as soon as he was elected, Pope Leo XIV escaped the fate of mere mortals. He left behind all his belongings as a snake sheds its first skin, even if this animal—which sometimes hangs around under apple trees—has had a bad reputation since the Book of Genesis. The white cassock he dons in the Chamber of Tears is not a reward, but rather a sign of renunciation, a radical renunciation. In other words, the new pope no longer belongs to himself. By changing his name, the man recently named Leo XIV has become Peter's successor, literally and figuratively. Did not Jesus promise the fisherman in Galilee that someone else would eventually guide him? 'Amen, amen, I say to you: when you were young, you girded yourself to go wherever you wanted; when you are old, you will stretch out your hands, and someone else will gird you, to take you where you do not want to go' (Jn 21:18). Pope Leo XIV was no longer solely concerned with the sheep of his diocese, which someone else was going to administer in his place. But he has taken on the shoulders of a multitude. He now had the care of the universal Church. This burden was truly inhuman and he could not carry it alone. Leo XIV counted on the grace of God, but also on a few faithful collaborators. In the weeks and months to come, they will carry out their duties with zeal, following the example of Simon of Cyrene, the man requisitioned to carry the cross of Jesus.

For the papacy is not exactly a sinecure. From the very first day of his pontificate, Leo XIV's desk was lined with piles of files of varying degrees of urgency. The scale of the task would not have been a surprise for the pope. He knows the Vatican and its inhabitants well: its climate, its greatness and its turpitude. He regularly came to take the temperature of the Tiber before returning home, to his own place. Now, his balcony overlooks St Peter's Square and the 1.4 billion Catholics who look to him. Some would say it's a beautiful view from the loggia of the basilica where he pronounced his first blessing *urbi et orbi* ('to the city and the world'). But this panorama overlooking the Via della Conciliazione, which links St Peter's Square to the Castel Sant'Angelo, can induce vertigo.

Francis was elected in 2013 to decentralise the Catholic Church towards the peripheries and reform the Vatican. And Leo XIV, what is he to do? Considering the scale of the task, he no doubt had to resist the temptation to throw in the towel. He is not the first pope—nor the last—to struggle against himself.

This is the moment to quote a famous apocryphal text entitled Acts of Peter. Peter left Rome, walking along the Appian Way, in fear of possible persecution. In short, he takes to the skies. He meets Jesus and asks him: *Quo vadis Domine*? ('Where are you going, Lord?'). This dialogue is so moving that it deserves to be read in full. Jesus replied: *Romam eo iterum crucifigi* ('I am going to Rome to be crucified again'). Peter asked him: 'Lord, will you be crucified again?' And the Lord said to him, 'Yes, I will be crucified again'. Peter changed his mind, regained his courage and returned to Rome, where he was immediately arrested and finally crucified upside down.

Fortunately, Pope Leo XIV has a good head on his shoulders. But he is aware that the Argentinian pontiff is leaving him with a lot of unfinished business. Francis has opened so many doors that many in the Curia are tired of the draughts. It is now up to Leo XIV to respond to the challenges for which he was chosen.

Imposing his Own Style

Leo XIV's first challenge is undoubtedly to find a way to succeed a Pope as disruptive as Francis, a pope popular even outside the Catholic world, but with an inimitable personality. 'It will be very difficult to succeed Pope Francis.' This thought was often heard in the corridors of the Vatican. Pope Leo XIV is now in that tight spot. 'The style is the man,' they say, and everyone is trying to discern the approach of the man whom the cardinal electors have just chosen. How can he move beyond the image conveyed by Francis? How can he embody the closeness and spontaneity that were his hallmarks? 'Each pope has his own style', warns Matthieu Rougé, Bishop of Nanterre. 'In their own way, John Paul II and Benedict XVI lacked neither simplicity nor sobriety. On a personal level, I'm very attached to the simplicity, which is always first and foremost fraternal, of relations within the Church and beyond. But, once again, this simplicity is not primarily an ascetic or moral point of attention, but the expression of an authentic rootedness in Christ.'

From Pope Leo XIV's first steps, we can already guess in which direction he wants to go. One thing is certain: he will not be a clone of Francis. Francis had his own style of communication. Sometimes criticised internally for giving so much room to improvisation and sentiment, Francis gave more than two hundred interviews to the media, sometimes impromptu and expressing himself without filters.

His press conferences on the plane were also marked by a great freedom of tone. Leo XIV must decide for himself whether or not he will return to a more academic and polished style of speaking, a more institutional style. Pope Francis has changed the image of the papacy by showing himself to be very close to the poor and the famous 'peripheries'. These are places far from decision-making centres where power, light and wealth are often concentrated. Francis also shared with the world his concern for inter-religious dialogue, particularly with Islam. He has taken the issue of the ecological crisis head-on, linking the protection of nature with social justice. Leo XIV must build on this legacy in the face of climate change and growing social inequalities around the world, which point to an intensification of migratory flows.

Francis was pro-active, a go-getter and had little concern for protocol. How will Pope Leo XIV make his mark? His predecessor gave the Vatican a tremendous boost. Since Paul VI, no pope had really looked after the governance of the Curia. He took charge in a way that is unusual in this milieu where silence is golden. In Rome, we still remember his 2014 greetings to the Curia, when he publicly criticised the cardinals, those who had taken the trouble to elect him. He lamented the spread of deadly 'diseases' among the men in red: 'spiritual Alzheimer's', 'gloomy faces', 'backbiting', 'gossip', 'worldly profit' and 'exhibitionism'. The man who was reluctant to come to Rome when he was Archbishop of Buenos Aires undertook, once in the Chair of Peter, to reform everything from top to bottom—even if it made the heads spin of those who could not comprehend the energy of this pope, the mover and shaker.

A Prophetic Voice in International Chaos

The choice of Pope Leo XIV is instructive in this respect. In the eyes of the cardinal electors, he embodies a voice capable of making itself heard in the current geopolitical chaos. For the first time, Francis denounced 'a world war being waged piecemeal.' But it has to be said that the situation has worsened since 2013. Today, new deadly conflicts are ravaging the planet, as in Ukraine and the Gaza Strip. World public opinion is expecting the new pope to do something decisive. But what can this man in white, head of a tiny state, where the Swiss guards have halberds rather than Kalashnikovs, do on his own?

The papacy is undaunted, because it also has special forces at its disposal: hidden, spiritual forces that hide in the shadow of monasteries or elsewhere, just about everywhere in the world. 'My kingdom is not of this world' (Jn 18:36), Jesus warned the powerful. For all that, Peter's successor has no intention of remaining a spectator to the global dramas unfolding in 2025. The fight for peace is a constant feature of the Vatican, even if the methods used vary according to the personalities of the popes. The Argentine Pope was renowned for promoting 'diplomacy against the grain'. He was capable of disconcerting gestures, as when he kissed the feet of the two leaders of South Sudan, to support his plea for peace in April 2019. The extraordinary image went round the world. Through this action, which surprised even his closest collaborators, Francis wanted to shine a spotlight on the tragic situation of a country that has known nothing but war since its creation in 2011. Whatever his pace and approach, Leo XIV will also have to carry this prophetic message from the Holy See. A weak force that often ends up bending those who are armed to the teeth.

It should be remembered that his predecessor never spared any effort, even if it meant being misunderstood. The proliferation of wars has been one of the heaviest crosses of Francis' pontificate. He placed great emphasis on the theme of reconciliation during delicate journeys, notably to Bosnia, the Central African Republic, Colombia, Burma, Iraq, the Democratic Republic of Congo and South Sudan. But his position has also been challenged in other areas.

The war in Ukraine, which began in 2014 in the Donbass region but spread to the whole country after the Russian offensive in February 2022, particularly mobilised him. He had made numerous unsuccessful appeals on behalf of 'martyred Ukraine', while at the same time receiving a great deal of criticism for his initial positions, which were perceived as being too neutral, or even smacking of appeasement towards Russia. His hopes of visiting both countries and taking on a mediation role proved to be in vain, and his tears of impotence during the Marian prayer on 8 December 2022 moved the whole world.

The war in Gaza, provoked by the Hamas offensive on Israel on 7 October 2023 and which triggered massive Israeli bombardments to which 50,000 Palestinians fell victim, also marked the end of the pontificate. 'By calling the parish in Gaza every evening, even when he was hospitalised and limited in his ability to speak, the Pope showed courage and helped to save hundreds of lives', said one cardinal. 'Because of the media attention that his appeals generated, this parish was one of the few places that the Israelis did not dare to bomb', he said, paying tribute to the pope's concern for this 'small flock'. Nevertheless, the Pope's voice did not prevent the war from continuing.

This burden of endless wars falls on Pope Leo XIV. Elected to carry the Gospel far and wide without recourse to the weapons of this world, he embodies this alternative and demanding voice that must resonate in a fractured geopolitics. 'We are in a context of war, with communities becoming isolated', points out Bishop Patrick Valdrini, a French canonist who has lived in Rome for many years. 'The sense of the common good is disappearing and political leaders have great expectations of the Church. We saw this at Francis' funeral.'

In truth, the aura of the Holy See has not waned. 'The lightning meeting between Donald Trump and Volodymyr Zelensky at St Peter's in Rome shows what the Church can contribute to certain conflicts', argues Guillaume Lagane, a professor at the Paris Institute of Political Studies. Seen from rue Saint-Guillaume in Paris, the diplomacy of the Holy See is something to dream about. It obeys a logic that runs counter to that of competition and violence. Who could have imagined the shocking image of the American President leaning towards his Ukrainian counterpart in the sublime, numinous void of the Papal Basilica? The content of their exchanges is unknown, but everyone will have noted that a historic agreement was signed between the two countries a few days later. After several months of negotiations, the two men agreed to exploit three strategic minerals: manganese, titanium and graphite.

That day, the alchemy of the Holy See came into full play. A mysterious combination of setting, solemnity of place and moment: the *kairos*, as the ancient Greeks used to say. 'This meeting made us forget the catastrophic image left by the meeting between the two men at the White House two months earlier', insists Guillaume Lagane. Donald Trump and Volodymyr Zelensky are not Catholic leaders, but they are caught up by Catholicism. For a specialist in international relations, it is striking to note that the Pope is an alternative agent when it comes to diplomacy. 'The United States was originally a great Protestant power. It only established diplomatic relations with the Holy See in the 1980s. But the paradox is that Catholicism now plays a major role in American politics.' The same reasoning could be applied to Zelensky. This political leader of Jewish descent, who leads a country with an Orthodox majority, also has to reckon with the Greek-Catholic minority that historically forms the crucible of Ukrainian nationalism.

The Church is therefore still capable of offering its good offices. 'This consists of organising a meeting in a favourable setting without offering a solution', explains Guillaume Lagane. In the absence of a magic wand, Pope Leo XIV is, by virtue of his very office, a great voice above the fray of partisan interests and dirty tricks between rival nations. His role is increasingly perilous. 'The new question facing the Pope today', says our professor, 'is how to position himself at a time when brute force is once again tending to become the norm in international relations. Stalin used to ask: "How many divisions does the Pope command?" Yet John Paul II was able to galvanise all those who were against communism, in the face of powers like Russia and China.'

Can the Vatican's *soft power* still play a role in the days to come? Some think so, even if they don't go to Mass every Sunday. Others—like dictators and their supporters—scorn this unarmed power. For it goes without saying that the Holy See is a completely separate international player in a world where relations are dictated by political and economic power. Contemporary popes, against winds and tides, have always succeeded in making this small voice heard against the current, whether by the panache of John Paul II breaching the Wall that divided Europe in two, or the concentrated gentleness of Benedict XVI in the face of Islamist threats.

Leo XIV looks towards Kiev and Moscow, of course. But also towards the Middle East, where the horrifying sound of bombing never ceases. 'Francis called for peace; he denounced the killing of civilians, but he limited himself moral dimension', says Guillaume Lagane. 'The Vatican had no practical solution to propose. Can the next Pope go further?' The international relations specialist has no crystal ball. But he knows that the whole world has high expectations of the Pope. People are counting on him to do the impossible. 'Nothing is impossible for God' (Lk 1:37), Jesus repeated to his incredulous apostles.

Confronting the Diktats of *Wokism* and the Challenge of Cultures

Francis had seen the storm coming. His successor Leo XIV began his pontificate at the height of the North American hurricane. In westernised countries, Judeo-Christian roots are being torn up by this new ideology, which believes that the difference between men and women is a question of culture, not nature. Inevitably, the questions are being asked more in the North than in the South. During the conclave, the cardinal electors no doubt returned to this anthropological war between continents that no longer share the same frames of reference. Cardinal Arborelius, from Stockholm, is like a lighthouse in the woke storm, a calm and solid captain who does not fear the height of the waves: 'The message of the Gospel is something eternal', he confided before the conclave. 'The same goes for the Catholic message on sexuality. If we can help people to understand that we are not just children of our time and culture, that can be very helpful. There are values and messages that transcend time and space.'

Rediscovering these values would be the best way of bridging the growing anthropological divide between continents. Pope Leo XIV is well aware of this. What is promoted in Los Angeles or Paris is not necessarily the same in Moscow or Ouagadougou. As the philosopher Blaise Pascal said: 'Truth within the Pyrenees, error beyond.' The new pontificate will inevitably be touched by this poison of relativism, where each person has his or her own truth. Pope Leo XIV is the guardian of the unity and the deposit of the faith, but he is confronted with increasingly antagonistic cultural universes. While the global North was greatly affected by the loss of anthropological landmarks stemming from Judeo-Christianity, the global South was resisting the westernisation of culture, albeit with some ambiguity. This geographical and religious divide was used by Moscow to justify the war in Ukraine. We remember the blunt words of Patriarch Kirill in 2022: 'There is a test of loyalty to [Western] power, a kind of pass to this "happy" world, a world of excessive consumption, a world of apparent "freedom". The test is very simple and at the same time terrifying: it's a gay pride parade.'

The new pope is not going to abandon Christian anthropology. However, he will have to find the right words and the right time to make himself understood. A member of the Roman Curia, well versed in ecumenism, explains: 'The anthropological divide cuts across the Churches. They are all affected: the Anglican Church, the Orthodox Church—most of whose faithful live in the United States—the Catholic Church with its reactions to the text *Fiducia supplicans* on the blessing of homosexual couples . . . For a long time', recalls this theologian, 'the divide was between East and West. The Cold War added to this division. But today, the divide has shifted between the North and the global South, which is developing more rapidly from a Christian point of view. Eastern Christians are also at odds with this Western anthropology, which violates moral and social norms.'

How can the pope deliver the same message in such diametrically opposed situations? 'There is a differentiated primacy of the Bishop of Rome', reassures our theologian. 'This was already the case in the first millennium. The Pope does not exercise his primacy in the same way over the Latin Churches or the Eastern Churches.' The same is true in different cultural contexts such as Black Africa. Cardinal Ratzinger—who could hardly be suspected of being progressive on this issue—stressed that the unitary vision of primacy was a fairly recent idea. We must undoubtedly distinguish the question of wokism from the necessary 'inculturation' of Christianity in different cultures, without lapsing into relativism. To hear some specialists in the Curia tell it, having everything managed from Rome in a homogenous way is not a model for the future, even when it comes to promoting Christian anthropology: 'We are moving towards a new decentralised balance that will call on the work of the bishops' conferences.'

The anthropological divide is not set in stone. And the worst is not certain. In the United States, there has been a 180-degree turn away from the temptation of wokism. This is surprising proof that major trends can be reversed. 'The Christians of Africa and the Middle East are also encouraging us in our Christian witness', says a French religious in a dicastery. 'We are becoming a minority Church in the West. This should encourage us to be more courageous in the face of social change.' For all that, the Churches of the South also face their own difficulties.

Mission in Good Times and Bad

When we talk about courage, the first thing that comes to mind is the courage of the martyrs in Africa and elsewhere. But we should not forget the courage, in old Europe, of those young missionaries who dare, in one way or another, to share their faith. They bear witness in a completely uninhibited way, without the embarrassment of their elders, or at least of a certain number of them who were concerned with a more 'hidden' mission. I would like to digress for a moment to recall a personal encounter with Pope Francis.

It was on 10 January 2025, with the leaders of the Mission Congress, an annual event designed to bring together all Catholics in France who are aware of the urgency of the mission. The sky was bright and the city of Rome almost deserted. Our small group was the only one huddled in front of St Peter's Basilica. Meeting the pope is a rare privilege, and those in charge of the Mission Congress were well aware of this. We were all novices, apart from two young up-and-coming personalities from the Church of France: Anne-Geneviève Montagne and Raphaël Cornu-Thénard, the instigators of this annual event, who had already met Francis in a private audience in 2020.

Some, like me, felt like they had won the Lotto. Providence often gives us this feeling of being fulfilled beyond our imagination—even when it is unbridled. The clock was ticking and our group was approaching the famous bronze gate and the Swiss guards with their red plumes. How could we fail to be struck by this atmosphere of Vatican majesty enhanced by the quiet magnificence of the architecture? After the bronze door, Pius IX's staircase and the courtyard of Saint Damasus . . . We all had the impression of being at the centre of the Church's turbine: a silent heart pulsing with invisible energy. Religious history buffs were in heaven. Our insignificant feet were treading on Sixtus V's palace. The most curious looked up to the top floor, which dates back to Clement VIII (Pope from 1592 to 1605). According to experts, this entrance was built by a certain Maderno around 1619. The awesome beauty of the building took our breath away, as did the magnificent staircase that brought us closer to the pope and the Consistory Hall.

We entered the immense Consistory Hall, with its gilded and carved wooden ceiling, dazzled. For some of us it seemed like a dream. It was as if we were outside time. And then came the long wait. The pope was meeting other French people in another room of the palace, 'brothers and sisters' from the diocese of Chartres. The French were everywhere this morning. At last the pope arrived, sliding back in his chair with a wry smile. He looked tired but serene. Would he have the strength to read his speech? The Holy Father gazed at our small assembly:

> 'I am delighted to meet you, you who are the faces and hearts of the Mission Congress. I thank you for your visit and above all for your faithful commitment to the service of the Gospel, which is a source of light and hope in a world that so desperately needs it.'

His background information was accurate. He knew that the organisers had had the boldness to book the Accor Arena: 'As you prepare for your major gathering at Bercy, the Church has just entered a new jubilee year that invites us to be "pilgrims of hope". It is an urgent call to renew our Christian life, which sends us on a mission: to become witnesses of a hope that never disappoints (*cf* Romans 5:5).' None of the French pilgrims were disappointed.

Francis continued his little exhortation, which came just at the right moment on this sunny morning:

> 'Dear friends, joy is inseparable from hope, and it is also inseparable from mission; a joy which is not reduced to the enthusiasm of the moment, but which is born of the encounter with Christ and which directs us towards our brothers and sisters [. . .] I encourage you never to be afraid of "setting out", because mission is a passion for Jesus. It means going where men and women live out their joys and their sorrows.'

He concluded: 'Thank you for all that you do, thank you for your dynamism and enthusiasm, for the missionary fraternity that you weave with patience and faith throughout France . . .' Francis paused for a moment. He said a few words in French: 'France, the eldest daughter of the Church. And the enemies of France say: "Yes, the eldest daughter of the Church, but not the most faithful . . .". It's not true! So many saints in France! So many saints!'

Readers will forgive this long anecdote, which simply illustrates the fact that the popes, since Vatican II, have never ceased to exhort Western Catholics to mission, and to the responsibility of making the Gospel known in a cultural space being eroded by secularisation. How can Pope Leo XIV today respond to the religious thirst evident in the new generations? The pontificate of Francis opened with the apostolic exhortation *Evangelii gaudium* on 'proclaiming the Gospel in today's world': A challenge that is two thousand years old, yet still burning and relevant for Peter's successor. We are obviously waiting for Pope Leo XIV to re-state these age-old truths in his own words.

Saint Peter, the first of the popes, already had a very clear message on this subject: 'Be ready at all times to present a defence to anyone who asks you to give an account of the hope that is in you, but do so with gentleness and respect' (1 Pet 3:15–16).

In an interview published in *La Croix* a few days before the conclave, the American theologian William Cavanaugh made this point forcefully:

> The greatest challenge is the desertion of the churches, not only in the global North, in Europe and North America, but also in Latin America. There is a huge drop in the number of people who identify themselves as Catholics and in the number of Catholics who go to church regularly. This is probably the greatest challenge for the next pope, combining a crisis of credibility with continuing secularisation, sociological upheaval and lifestyle changes.

In a way, that says it all about the unfathomable challenge facing Leo XIV.

What can the new Pope do in the face of secularisation? He will not cast anathemas on the West. Leo XIV is not like the Persian king Xerxes I who, in the 3rd century BCE, had the sea whipped furiously to punish it for having thwarted his plans in the Dardanelles Straits. He had imagined building a bridge between the two shores with his ships, but the stormy seas dashed his hopes. The pope obviously has an entirely different philosophy. For all that, he knows that the pontificate of Francis has not halted secularisation in the West, a long-standing and complex phenomenon that is manifesting itself in the Catholic Church through a steady decline in vocations. In the space of ten years, from 2011 to 2021, Europe has seen a decline of 27,000 priests, 6,000 seminarians and almost 80,000 nuns. Of course, the Pope could take comfort in the fact that Africa and Asia have seen an increase in the number of priests over this period: 52,000 priests in Africa compared with 39,000 ten years previously. But the Pope is perfectly aware that this is not enough to compensate for the drop in vocations globally. Even more worrying is the fact that even in Asia, a continent favoured by Francis, the number of seminarians has fallen under his pontificate (down 9% from 2011 to 2021). Is Leo XIV defeated? No, because behind the weight of the figures, there is always grace.

While continuing the Argentine pontiff's impetus towards the peripheries, Leo XIV's task will be to remobilise Catholicism in the old countries with a Catholic tradition. Against this difficult backdrop, a strong upturn in adult and youth baptisms in France and the UK has aroused surprise and interest from Rome. 'Something is happening in France. It may be the first sign of a new springtime for the Church', rejoiced a cardinal of the Roman Curia who is very close to Pope Francis.

Although old Europe has long ceased to be the locomotive of the faith, its embers continue to glow. A number of cardinal electors were struck by what happened recently in France. This is the conviction that Cardinal Schönborn OP expressed to a number of French journalists on the eve of the conclave:

> 'Christians must stop lamenting the decline of Europe or waiting for a restoration of Christianity. What is our fundamental Christian conviction? The Lord is risen. He is still at work today. The 18,000 adult baptisms that took place this year in France are a sign. So is the resurrection of Notre-Dame de Paris. We have to know how to read these signs of the times.'

The eldest daughter of the Church, even when tired, remains an example for the universal Church to ponder. She encourages the old Christian countries not to let themselves die of despair. The inspired homily given by Cardinal Artime, former Prefect of the Dicastery for Institutes of Consecrated Life and Societies of Apostolic Life, on the occasion of the *Novemdiales*, on 3 May, is worth noting. We were still in the period when the cardinals prayed for the repose of the soul of the deceased pope. The cardinal highlighted the 'absence of God' felt in contemporary societies. He recalled how Pope Francis was asking religious to be signs of 'prophecy' in the face of the '*areopagi* of a world without God'.

We can imagine that Pope Leo XIV is not afraid of secularisation. He was right to the extent that this phenomenon, however massive, is showing signs of weakness. At the end of secularisation, there is nothing but a dead end. This is the opinion of Bishop Patrick Valdrini, who has worked for many years in the Roman Curia: 'Our Western civilisation invents new rights every day without reminding us of our duties', emphasises the canonist. 'In our secularised societies, seekers of meaning expect something else from us! They are looking for a third party who can remind them of their duties and convey an ethical message based on transcendence.' This can only be the conviction of the new pope. 'In the Church, the community is not the sum of individuals. Its unity comes from God and it symbolises what God wants for the whole of humanity.' For this keen observer, the coming pontificate will remind us of this truth in one way or another.

'[Community] is the best antidote to individualism. The young people who knock on the door of the churches have had very powerful personal experiences. Then they discover the importance of community.'

But one might legitimately ask whether the Pope should give priority to Catholics or to people of goodwill, or even to those from other religious traditions. 'The priority', insists Matthieu Rougé, Bishop of Nanterre,

> is never to oppose what should be united. We need to proclaim Jesus Christ, true God and true man, to the faithful and to catechumens, so that they can grow in their faith, and to all those who do not know him, so that they can discover him. We also need to deepen ecumenical work, dialogue with Judaism, inter-religious dialogue and fraternal encounters with all. The catholicity of the Church is expressed in the universality of its mission. The priority of the Bishop of Rome is to be the witness and servant of this universality of salvation.

An irreplaceable mission.

A Synodal Path Strewn with Pitfalls

While the pope is immediately awaited *ad extra*, on the vast stage of the world, he will inevitably be scrutinised with regard to several hot issues specific to Catholics. The first is undoubtedly that of governance in the Church. The place of women immediately springs to mind. Francis had raised great expectations, which were sometimes disappointed. He had made some strong gestures, such as the first appointment of a woman, Sister Simona Brambilla, to head a dicastery in January 2025. It is true that the various synods organised under Francis' pontificate—these large assemblies for reflection on the family, young people or the specific challenges of

Amazonia— sometimes gave the impression of a certain confusion. We had the impression that the Catholic Church was operating at different speeds, particularly on the very sensitive issues of priestly celibacy, homosexuality and access to communion for divorced people who had remarried. At the beginning of 2024, the African bishops' opposition to the *Fiducia supplicans* declaration opening the way to blessings for people living as same-sex couples revealed the deep divisions on these issues.

That said, the synod is not a modernist invention. It is a traditional reality dating back to Christian antiquity. 'It is a question of walking together with God, under his watchful eye', Francis insisted, without always being understood. While there is something simple and exciting about these conversations in the Spirit, it has been difficult for the general public to see the concrete results. Since 2021, the process of the 'Synod on Synodality'—a complex code name that has brought a smile to the face of many Catholics in France and elsewhere—has set itself the task of exploring, without taboos, themes such as the governance of the Church and co-responsibility between priests and lay people. The place of women in the Church was also at the heart of the reflections. But the question of the female diaconate was not resolved, due to a lack of consensus. By choosing not to publish an apostolic exhortation at the end of the last synod, Pope Francis has left it to his successor to make decisions on some very burning issues. One thing is certain: the future Pope will not be able to sweep Francis' spirit of reform under the carpet.

For Leo XIV, synodality is one of the few items already on his agenda, along with the Jubilee 2025 celebrations. During his hospitalisation, Francis was keen to defer the synodal calendar until 2028. Francis' successor is well aware that the pre-synodal meetings may have given rise to clashes between generations and sensitivities. 'Because of a lack of time, motivation or the ability to engage in respectful dialogue, small, homogenous groups met among themselves without opening up to the full breadth of ecclesial communion', says Bishop Matthieu Rougé, who took part in the 2023 and 2024 synods. 'As always in the life of the Church, it is by going deeper that we can overcome ecclesial tensions.' Once again, the worst is never certain. For Jesuit theologian Christoph Theobald, the experience of the synod appears to be very positive, and he sees in it a form of 'council that does not speak its name'.

Is the process initiated by Francis irreversible? 'The vocabulary of "irreversibility" does not seem to me to be adapted either to historical realities in general or to ecclesial realities in particular', Bishop Rougé points out. 'The history of the Church is a life that develops, goes back and forth, and deepens, without any one period being able to set itself up as an unsurpassable reference point.' He adds that form should not take precedence over content: 'Synodality, as Pope Francis has called for its renewal, is all the more interesting and promising because it will not be set up as an absolute starting point or revolution.'

It goes without saying that the synodal path opened by Francis cannot be closed. But his successor is expected to clarify a number of burning issues. Some observers are worried that the Catholic Church is becoming fragmented, with doctrinal differences crystallising from one continent to another. For the Bishop of Nanterre, these tensions should not call into question the fruitfulness of this process: 'I was very impressed to see that, beyond certain clashes or ideological agendas, the mystery of the Church, in all its beauty, breadth and depth, peacefully imposed itself as the right framework within which to promote this or that desirable development.' However, synodality is not a magic formula: 'It is not so much synodality that revitalises Christianity as authentic rootedness in Christ that can bring synodality to life', he warns.

Continuing the Reform of the Curia

Of all the challenges faced by Pope Leo XIV, there is one that must be taken seriously, because it is undermining the universal Church's ability to act and the atmosphere in Rome. I am talking about the reform of the Curia. *Ecclesia semper reformanda* is the Latin saying: 'The Church is always in need of reform.' This is a truth that Leo XIV cannot forget. All the more so since the cardinal electors who chose him expect him to follow through on the efforts undertaken by Francis. With his own rhythm and method, of course.

During his pontificate, Pope Francis led an ambitious programme of reforms aimed at rethinking the workings of the Roman Curia, the administrative heart of the Catholic Church. His aim was to make the Holy See more open to the world, more transparent and more modern, at the service of the dioceses. This reform finally led to the promulgation of a new apostolic constitution, *Prædicate Evangelium*, in 2022. But what's next?

Francis' proactive approach came up against a number of obstacles, starting with internal resistance. Controversial decisions on human resources management have also generated a feeling of unease among employees in recent years.

While the pope has cleaned up the books, he has not managed to put the financial situation on a sustainable footing: the Vatican remains structurally in deficit, due in particular to the decline in donations from the faithful, which is affecting its pension fund in particular.

A member of the Curia confided off the record on the eve of the conclave: 'We don't know how to do fund raising! All we have to do is reply to one of the American production companies begging to be allowed to film in the Sistine Chapel: It's €2 million for the rental. But we don't dare.'

The financial scandal surrounding the 'London building affair', which led to Cardinal Angelo Becciu being sentenced to five and a half years in prison, appears ambivalent: it has highlighted a certain persistent lack of transparency in the Vatican's financial management, while at the same time revealing the pope's desire to put an end to a system undermined by nepotism and amateurism.

Many Vatican sources agree that the next Pope will have to 'oil the machine' by continuing the reforms, but without bullying or humiliating the staff. This will be no easy task for Leo XIV.

Calming the Liturgical Quarrel

Seen from France or the United States, this is a particularly delicate issue. It is hard to say, but the wound inflicted by the schism with Archbishop Lefebvre, in response to some of the more or less bizarre applications of the Second Vatican Council, has never been healed. Popes have tried to heal the mortal wound of traditionalism. But none has succeeded in closing the wound once and for all.

Leo XIV will have to perform advanced surgery, for Francis has left behind a deadlocked situation. On 16 July 2021, a thunderclap rocked a serene sky: the Pope promulgated the motu proprio *Traditionis custodes*, drastically limiting the use of the pre-conciliar Tridentine rite. Francis thus explained his decision to reverse a decision taken by his predecessor Benedict XVI: he was concerned about the 'growing rejection of the liturgical reform' among some Catholics and, more broadly, of the Second Vatican Council.

Traditionis custodes provoked a heated debate in the traditionalist world. On 11 February 2022, Francis signed a decree exempting the priests of the Priestly Fraternity of St Peter from the provisions of this *motu proprio*. While other communities and parishes waited for the decree to be extended, the mothers of priests, united in an association, brought the pontiff more than two thousand letters from Catholics asking for the restrictions to be lifted. In December 2021, the Dicastery for Divine Worship and the Discipline of the Sacraments responded to eleven *dubia*—objections or requests for clarification made by bishops—that had been submitted to it, confirming a strict interpretation of the motu proprio. In his speeches, Francis regularly lambasted traditionalists, accusing them of advocating a 'return to the past' and labelling them with a 'dead faith'.

In a final blow to those hoping for greater flexibility, the pope reaffirmed the authority of the Holy See in a rescript published on 21 February 2023. Since that date, bishops have had to request authorisation from the Roman dicastery to allow a priest ordained after the promulgation of *Traditionis custodes* to celebrate with the 1962 Roman Missal, as well as to use a parish church wishing to host the Tridentine Mass.

What will Pope Leo XIV do? The new head of the Church will no doubt be keen not to add fuel to the fire, without disowning Francis. This balancing act is important for the life of the Church, as explained by Jean-Pierre Batut, the auxiliary bishop of Toulouse, who was once in charge of the bi-ritualist parish of Saint-Eugène-Sainte-Cécile in Paris: 'When we use the liturgy as an instrument, we turn the place of communion into a place of division, as Saint Paul already deplored. ("I I hear that when you all come together as a community, there are separate factions among you", 1 Cor 11:18). In so doing, we are tearing the tunic of Christ!' According to him, this was not simply a question of liturgical sensitivity. Francis couldn't see how one could recognise the validity of Vatican II and at the same time not accept the liturgical reform resulting from the Council. It has to be said that at that time, as Bishop Batut explains, anarchy was the order of the day:

> My generation saw the transition to the new Order of Mass. We didn't receive any training, as if we were born with it . . . That was the cause of many abuses at the time. The celebrants hadn't read Paul VI's presentation of the new Roman Missal. They immediately went off at a tangent. In the training they

> had received at the seminary, the liturgy consisted simply of following the rubrics. And when the rubrics changed, some priests imagined that they could do whatever came into their heads! Francis wanted to combat this unbearable distortion.

The blame seems to be shared in this complex affair: 'What Benedict XVI generously granted', summarises Bishop Batut, 'some have unfortunately made questionable use of. From permission for the Mass, we've moved on to all the sacraments, the Liturgy of the Hours and the refusal to make the texts of the Council known. In other words, Benedict XVI's charity has not always been faithfully received. It's a pity that those who have shown loyalty to Rome are paying the price.'

It is an opinion shared by Dom Geoffroy Kemlin, current Father Abbot of the Abbey of Solesmes:

> There is a middle ground to be maintained in liturgical celebration. 'Anything goes' disfigures the celebration and prevents it from making visible the beauty of Christ and the salvation he brings. But too scrupulous a respect for the rubrics, or rather an exclusive focus on the rubrics, means that those celebrating overlook what they are celebrating.

The challenge for Pope Leo XIV is therefore to free the liturgy from excessively human and political quarrels, because beyond the liturgical dimension itself, the conflict is above all about the acceptance of the major texts of Vatican II: think in particular of the Declaration on Religious Freedom *Dignitatis humanae*, judged to be relativistic in the eyes of Archbishop Lefebvre's followers.

A Reminder that Ecology is not a Luxury

Leo XIV has a rich heritage in this area. By publishing the encyclical *Laudato si'* (2015), Francis showed the world the Holy See's attention to 'integral ecology'. More than just a fashion statement, it was a cry for the preservation of Creation. For Francis, our 'common home' is burning. It was not just an image for him, but a climatic reality reflected in statistics, and he wanted to measure its practical and spiritual implications. This is the *raison d'être* of *Laudato si'*. Rarely has a papal text found such an echo outside the Catholic world. The French environmental activist Maxime de Rostolan was received by the Pope, along with Bishop Éric de Moulins-Beaufort, President of the Episcopal Conference of France. For Francis, ecology was an extremely serious challenge with metaphysical overtones. For Maxime de Rostolan, 'these meetings were an opportunity to show that we could carry the same message together: the need to preserve our common home. They were also an opportunity to show environmental activists that spirituality is part of the solution.' Leo XIV cannot avoid taking up the theme of the climate crisis, which has an obvious spiritual dimension.

Will it take time for the new Pope to go 'green'? Time will tell, but Cardinal Bergoglio himself needed an 'ecological conversion'. In 2007, at the Latin American Bishops' Conference in Aparecida, Brazil, the Archbishop of Buenos Aires was unaware of the ecological issues at stake: 'I used to say, "But these Brazilians are tiring us out with this Amazonia! What has the Amazon got to do with evangelisation? [. . .]" I didn't understand anything!' In doing so, the man who was to become Pope Francis embraced the Holy See's commitment to the environment. Paul VI was the first pope to make an articulate speech on the environment. John Paul II devoted many speeches to ecology, as did Benedict XVI.

But Francis has moved up a gear. This was not 'the recent whim of a pope fresh from the pampas wanting to ride the green wave simply for the sake of marketing', says Dominican Thomas Michelet. In the eyes of the Argentine Pope, the environmental crisis was inseparable from an anthropological crisis. Francis felt he was following in the footsteps of Leo XIII when he had published the prophetic encyclical *Rerum novarum* on the working world. He accepted the notion of urgency, while avoiding apocalyptic rhetoric.

On the strength of his position, Francis launched a cry to the world. 'This cannot go on', he regularly repeated in his messages, such as the one sent to mark COP26 in Glasgow in November 2021. The Pope also hosted several initiatives at the Vatican, such as meetings with the heads of the world's largest energy groups (in 2018 and 2019), whom he urged to make a 'radical' energy transition. Finally, together with Orthodox Patriarch Bartholomew of Constantinople, he established the World Day of Prayer for the Integrity of Creation, celebrated each year on 1 September.

Far beyond ecological militancy, Francis called for a personal conversion. We are still a long way from achieving this, and Leo XIV knows it. In this matter, as in so many others, the essential work remains to be done. As Father Thomas Michelet so aptly put it: 'Conversion of eyes and ears, to see and hear this distress to which we remain deaf and blind. Conversion of head and heart, to discern the deep root of the evil within us that affects Creation. Conversion of the hands, which must no longer always appropriate and destroy, but offer and share, build and protect, bless and praise.'

The Fight Against Sexual and Spiritual Abuse

Another key issue for Leo XIV is the highly sensitive question of sexual and spiritual abuse in the Church. The abuse crisis was one of the central themes of the 2013 conclave. It would also be discussed at length during the 2025 conclave, according to Vatican experts.

Francis' successor must therefore continue—and above all put into practice—the principles already solemnly laid down by the Church. 'The texts denouncing the abhorrent nature of sexual and spiritual abuse already exist', points out Archbishop Patrick Valdrini. 'The decision has been taken at the highest level.' This French canonist is referring to the motu proprio *Vos estis lux mundi*, which from 2019 sets out provisions for combating sexual abuse.

In March 2014, Francis created a Pontifical Commission for the Protection of Minors. But its work was tarnished by the departure of several of its members, who were disappointed by the lack of collaboration from the Roman Curia. The new Pope will also have to overcome the numerous scandals linked to sexual abuse, such as the general resignation of the bishops of Chile and the dismissal of Cardinal McCarrick, Archbishop Emeritus of Washington, from the clerical state, not to mention the calamitous revelations about key figures in the Church, such as Abbé Pierre and former Jesuit Marko Rupnik.

The new pontiff therefore has the tough task of continuing the fight against abuse, particularly in Africa and Asia. 'Implementation will have to be culturally sensitive', insists Archbishop Valdrini. 'It will be up to the bishops' conferences to put things in place.' At the risk of a multi-speed Church? 'The life of the Church will have to adapt its resources to cultures. If such and such a Church in black Africa decides to launch a CIASE tomorrow [CIASE is the French Church's Independent Commission on Sexual Abuse]. no one will come! Who would dare recount such facts of life? Who would risk being stoned to death by society? In other words, firmness will have to be accompanied by a good dose of education. The next Pope', adds Bishop Valdrini, 'could legally publish a letter for the Churches of Africa and Asia, stressing the need for a complete clean-up of the Church's stables, following the example of the process initiated in Europe. But in applying the law, there is always a judgement of expediency. We need to be discerning. The new Pope must ask himself: will voluntary efforts solve the problem or make it worse?'

This message is difficult to hear in our latitudes. Transparency and zero tolerance are not enough to solve all the problems. Far from it.

'In the past, the law spoke in Latin of *prudentia* and *aequitas*', recalls Bishop Valdrini. Equity is justice rendered on the basis of the good of the individual, not the institution. In law, the immediate application of principles takes into account the good of individuals. In France, we have lost the sense of equity in favour of a theoretical sense of justice. In the tradition of the Church, fairness is God himself and the way he treats people. He concludes: 'Above all, the Church must give itself the means to support victims. So much remains to be done.'

The issue of abuse has been with Father Prevost for a long time. Twenty years later, during his two years at the head of the Augustinian province of Our Lady of Good Counsel (1999–2001), he was strongly criticised by the American press over a case of sexual abuse of minors involving a member of his congregation. In September 2000, as provincial, at the request of the diocese, Father Prevost had given his agreement to the reception of a diocesan priest—who had been accused of several cases of abuse of minors and who was under surveillance—into an Augustinian priory located near a primary school.

It was only in 2002, with the tightening of the rules established by the American episcopate, that this priest was removed from this residence, before being laicised in 2012.

More recently, in March 2025, Cardinal Prevost came under renewed attack, this time from SNAP (Survivors Network of those Abused by Priests), accusing him of having carried out 'actions and omissions designed to interfere with or avoid a civil or canonical, administrative or criminal investigation against certain priests of the Diocese of Chiclayo'. A letter sent by this organisation to Cardinal Parolin, the Holy See's Secretary of State at the time, was reportedly never followed up. In 2023, the Diocese of Chiclayo commented on the affair, disputing the accusations point by point.

As Prefect of the Dicastery for Bishops, Cardinal Prevost was responsible for applying the rules of Pope Francis' motu proprio *Vos estis lux mundi*, which can lead to the resignation of bishops found guilty of negligence, covering up or mishandling cases of abuse involving priests under their jurisdiction.

Immediately after the pontifical election, two specialist organisations, SNAP and Bishop Accountability, issued press releases questioning the commitment of Robert Francis Prevost, the 69-year-old American prelate, to lift the veil on this scourge. As head of the Augustinian order worldwide, and then as bishop of the Peruvian diocese of Chiclayo between 2015 and 2023, 'he has not published a single name' of a guilty party, said Anne Barrett Doyle on behalf of Bishop Accountability.

Rather than respond to the various and sundry accusations that are still likely to rain down, Leo XIV must show his quiet determination in this matter.

What About Inter-Religious Dialogue?

By taking the name of Francis, Jorge Bergoglio undoubtedly intended to revive the memory of the saint of Assisi, who in the Middle Ages did not hesitate to enter into dialogue with the sultan in a spirit of peace. It is therefore easier to understand why one of the main thrusts of his pontificate, dialogue with Islam, has reached an unprecedented level with him, whereas relations with Muslims had come to a real standstill after the misunderstandings linked to Benedict XVI's Regensburg speech in 2006. In a decade marked by Islamist terrorism and the cruelty of Daech in the Middle East, the Pope has stepped up his meetings with Muslim dignitaries. His credo: the culture of encounter is the only alternative to 'the barbarity of those who breathe hatred' he explained at a peace conference organised at Al-Azhar University in Egypt in 2017.

In February 2019, this compass led him to Abu Dhabi (United Arab Emirates), where he sealed a historic agreement with Ahmed Al-Tayyeb, Grand Imam of Al-Azhar. Together, the two men signed an unprecedented document, *On Human Brotherhood*, a veritable compendium of common values to be defended by all religions, intended to be given to all influential leaders.

Pope Francis' third encyclical, *Fratelli tutti*, in turn represents a decisive step forward in dialogue. In it, he quotes Ahmed Al-Tayyeb several times—who, the Pope says, inspired the encyclical—and renews his call for all religions to condemn the violence committed in their name. He met up with his 'brother' Al-Tayyeb for the sixth time in five years during a trip to Bahrain in 2022. Meanwhile, in 2021, by meeting Ayatollah al-Sistani in Iraq, the Pope demonstrated his desire for dialogue with Shiite Islam. It was with this in mind that he named Dominique Mathieu, Archbishop of Tehran, a cardinal in December 2024.

Will Leo XIV continue along this path of dialogue? We should not hide the fact that this option has given rise to many questions, and even opposition. According to some, by favouring such an attitude, Pope Francis has shown a certain naivety. Did he not run the risk of sinking into a kind of religious indifference or confusion?

When he organised the Assisi prayer gathering in 1986, Pope John Paul II also received similar criticism from prominent members of the Curia. However, we must not forget that this openness to the sons of Abraham, Jews and Muslims is a requirement defied by the Second Vatican Council in its declaration *Nostra aetate*. We must remember that this is not just a pious wish, but a concern to build a spiritual and fraternal bond between people.

In today's turbulent world, it is a burning obligation to remind people that violence and fanaticism can only lead to dead ends. Is it by chance that the last words of Pope Francis were to condemn, in the same declaration, the massacre in Gaza and anti-Semitism? Leo XIV cannot escape this path, even if it often lies on a knife-edge.

The Ecumenical Imperative

This is one of the great images of Francis' pontificate. On 12 February 2016, almost a thousand years after the great schism of 1054, the head of the Catholic Church met the Orthodox Patriarch of Moscow for the first time. This historic meeting, which took place at Cuba airport, confirmed the warming of relations between the two Churches.

However, the policy of rapprochement came to a halt when, on 24 February 2022, Russian troops invaded Ukraine, with the blessing of Patriarch Kirill. Just as the Pope and the Patriarch were planning to meet in Jerusalem in June of the same year, the disagreements generated by the war in Ukraine came to light, with Pope Francis asking Kirill not to become 'Putin's altar boy'.

This setback in the history of relations with the Russian Orthodox is undoubtedly one of Pope Francis' greatest regrets. Leo XIV will have to pay close attention to this deadlock, at a time when many Ukrainian Orthodox have broken with Moscow.

On a completely different front, in 2016 Pope Francis travelled to Stockholm, Sweden, to mark the 500th anniversary of the Lutheran Reformation. Together with representatives of the Lutheran World Federation, he signed a joint declaration calling for a move beyond the 'conflicts of the past' towards greater communion and solidarity.

In 2018, as part of an 'ecumenical pilgrimage', he travelled to Geneva, Switzerland, to celebrate the 70th anniversary of the World Council of Churches. The organisation brings together 348 Orthodox, Protestant and Anglican churches and represents 500 million faithful.

Francis' style and personality have also led him to forge close relationships with his Christian brothers and sisters, in particular Patriarch Bartholomew of Constantinople, with whom he has met on ten occasions and who inspired his encyclical *Laudato si'*, and the Archbishop of Canterbury, Justin Welby, with whom he has worked in particular to resolve the conflict in South Sudan.

At the end of 2023, the publication of *Fiducia supplicans*, a declaration authorising Catholic priests to bless same-sex couples, revealed deep disagreements among the Christian Churches. In particular, it triggered the anger of the Copts, who announced that they were suspending their theological dialogue with the Catholic Church.

The path of ecumenical dialogue may therefore appear narrow for Leo XIV. How can we not work towards unity without entering into rivalry or competition? This is particularly true in the countries of the South, where evangelical communities are very dynamic, even proselytising. How can we also position ourselves on questions of morality, where there are strong differences of opinion between denominations? While the synodal approach is seen as largely positive by many Reformed Christians, it is not without its critics, who are concerned about a lapse into doctrinal diversity in the Catholic Church.

The image of the pontifical office has greatly improved among evangelical movements thanks to the consideration they have received from Pope Francis. Many misunderstandings have been resolved and convergences are emerging, particularly on moral issues. Prominent pastors, such as the Reverend Franklin Graham, have expressed their appreciation of being able to count on a voice that represents all Christians. Evangelical and Pentecostal churches, whose world is very much influenced by American culture, will certainly feel at ease with Leo XIV.

We received the reaction of French journalist Christine Kelly, who makes no secret of her evangelical Christian faith.

> The election of this new Pope is a very important moment for me. As soon as it was announced, I called my ten-year-old daughter. I pulled her towards me: 'Come on, let's sit down in front of the TV. That's it! *Habemus papam*, my girl! This is a historic moment. Whether you're Catholic or not. The whole family has sat down in front of the screen. I'm not Catholic, but this Pope is breathing new life into my faith. I noted his first words. I saw the look on his face. He was overwhelmed. And when he said, 'Peace be with you all', I shuddered. Those were the words of Jesus before he ascended into heaven. And I said to myself: this man is a true disciple of Christ.

For Christine Kelly, 'the Pope is the only voice today that can be heard throughout the world, proclaiming peace. In all other religions, there are many voices. But here, there is only one pastor, one word. It's unique. No head of state proclaims peace everywhere, at all times, for everyone.' And the Protestant journalist enthuses: 'Even if he's not my "pope", he inspires me. This pope brings joy, hope and confidence. And he makes us want to believe.'

The Weight of the Global South

Today, the Catholic house needs to be solid, because the support of the past has disappeared. 'The world has moved enormously in recent years', confides Cardinal Christoph Schönborn OP. We have entered a 'post-Western' world. A page is being turned in the life of the Church. The page was turned at the end of the Roman Empire when the barbarians took over. It turned over again in the wake of the Protestant Reformation and the Industrial Revolution. But only great minds—like the Archbishop Emeritus of Vienna—are capable of measuring the scale of the change underway. Without fear or naivety.

We ask him what the backdrop was to the discussions in the congregations behind closed doors. The legacy of Francis, the synodal path, abuses, Vatican finances, and so on. All this was present and sometimes obsessive. But the essential thing was elsewhere. There was something floating in the air, the feeling that we were experiencing a change of era. It is precisely this change that the new pope will have to negotiate. He will be a bridge between two eras.

In the eyes of the Austrian cardinal, all the immense challenges facing Peter's successor can be summed up in one: 'The global North is losing its importance in the Church and throughout the world. A shift is taking place towards the global South. For me, this is the great sign of our times.' The pontificate that is about to begin will inevitably take account of this movement of plate tectonics. 'This phenomenon does not just concern the Church', insists the Austrian cardinal. 'Just think that Africa will soon have two billion inhabitants. Europe maintains its population through immigration, not through its birth rate. The continent of Europe is changing simply because of demographics. Some predict that Europe will account for 4% of the world's population by 2050!'

The Cardinals know that to talk about the future of the Church, you have to talk about the future of the world. The two are inevitably intertwined. It's not a sin to know how to read the figures and make serious forecasts. New wine, new wineskins, as the Gospel says. 'It's not a question of being for or against', says the Austrian cardinal. 'These are facts. Just look at the liturgies in St Peter's Basilica. Who are the acolytes, the priests who distribute communion? They are not Europeans. Let's not forget that the papacy, in the 8th century, had Syrian popes. It was no longer the Roman Empire, which had disappeared. They came from the East . . .'

And what if the pontificate of Leo XIV was placed under the sign of the Magi who followed a mysterious star to find the Messiah? They didn't stay 'on their sofa', as Francis would have said. They started walking. But what is this star crossing the sky in 2025? 'The world's new balances are not minor elements', explains Cardinal Schönborn with his slight Central European accent. 'The issue of global justice will be central for the new Pope. I'm talking about Africa, which has been shamelessly exploited for generations with the help of certain African elites . . . Injustice in the global South is a source of conflict. All this might seem far removed from our faith. But Catholics live their faith in a concrete era. Our times are marked by a "third world war in pieces"', he says, using an expression coined by Pope Francis.

Does this mean that the election of the future Pope will mark the abandonment of the West to its sad fate? Cardinal Schönborn does not think so. He refers to Pope Benedict XVI's trip to the Czech Republic. 'Some people asked him why he was wasting his time visiting the most secularised country in Europe? He spoke of the religious thirst he had sensed.'

Benedict XVI said:

> In modern times, faith and hope have been displaced, relegated to the level of private life, as themes from another world. European Christians are therefore called upon to redouble their efforts to try to rediscover reasons to believe and hope, to emerge from their spiritual torpor, to rediscover the Christian memory of the continent. Christianity has a lot to offer a Europe that has been diminished in its perspectives.

An American Pope?

The Americans found it hard to believe at first. Could one of their compatriots really ascend the throne of Peter? Patrick Kelly, like many Americans, couldn't imagine it. In the eyes of the Supreme Knight of the Knights of Columbus, the world's largest Catholic charitable organisation, the prospect didn't seem very rational:

> 'The prevailing thinking for a long time was that a pope could never come from the United States. We are a powerful country, and for many, the idea of an American pope simply seemed excessive. Most Americans had resigned themselves to the belief that it would never happen, at least not in our lifetime. And yet it did.'

There was something unthinkable about the election of Leo XIV. Patrick Kelly remembers: 'I had the privilege of meeting him twice. He knows us. He respects us. And he cares about what we do. I'm convinced that we'll have a great relationship with him, and one of my essential duties now will be to nurture that bond even further.' He added: 'I remember the last time we met, in June 2023. He's a very approachable man—warm, attentive, fully present. He takes his time.

We talked about the importance of forming Catholic men, reaching out to them, helping them to live their faith. And he understood immediately. For him, the Church's mission is both pastoral and concrete.' He continues: 'When I saw him appear on the loggia yesterday, I was initially taken aback—an American pope! But what touched me most was the tone of his first message. He spoke of peace: "May peace be in all our hearts". And then he said something that made a deep impression on me: "We are a Church on the move"'.

Patrick Kelly is looking forward to seeing Leo XIV again in Rome. For the time being, he makes no secret of his delight at the idea of this nascent pontificate:

> I see in this choice a beautiful continuity, not only between North America and Latin America, but also with Europe. Pope Leo XIV is certainly American by birth, he grew up in Chicago and studied in Philadelphia and Villanova, but his decades of missionary work in Peru and his duties in Rome have made him a profoundly universal figure. He knows Latin America. He has a heart for the poor. And his responsibilities as Superior General of the Augustinians and then Prefect of the Dicastery for Bishops have brought him into contact with the Church in all its diversity. He is a man who unites worlds—North and South, local and universal, tradition and reform—in a single singular vocation. It's truly extraordinary.

Discreet but powerful, the Knights of Columbus are considered to be an essential part of the Catholic Church in the United States. Patrick Kelly intends to give Leo XIV the gift of his rare ability to mobilise human, financial and political resources, while remaining faithful to a resolutely Christian vision of the world.

He reflects on the name chosen by the pope:

> The choice of 'Leo' is deeply symbolic. Leo XIII is widely recognised as the father of modern Catholic social doctrine. His encyclicals, at the dawn of the industrial age, offered a balanced, courageous vision—a legacy admired by both left and right. Pope Leo XIV was not a man of political camps. He is a bridge-builder. He extends the vision of Leo XIII into our present day, just as John Paul II did with his encyclical *Centesimus annus*, published in 1991 to mark the centenary of *Rerum novarum*.

In short, this name is a whole programme, which Patrick Kelly outlines:

> As an American, I think that Pope Leo XIV will bring a certain clarity and a sense of organisation to the Roman Curia. In the coming months, I expect him to evaluate many of the people and processes in place, and to make thoughtful changes where necessary. This concern for structure—perhaps an American trait—will be invaluable to him.

In fact, Leo XIV spoke about the choice of his name over dinner with the cardinals after his election. 'The Pope wanted to situate his pontificate in the context of the "digital revolution"', said Cardinal Ladislav Nemet, Archbishop of Belgrade, who shared the Pope's table on the evening of 8 May 2025. The Serbian cardinal told Croatian broadcaster HRT: 'His name is his programme. At the dinner, Leo XIV explained that he had chosen this name in order to "give more attention to social issues in the world, and to issues of justice."' The previous pope who bore this name, Leo XIII (1810–1903), was considered to be the pope of the workers. 'He also said that we are in the midst of a new revolution. In Leo XIII's time, it was the industrial revolution, now we're in the middle of the digital revolution', added Cardinal Nemet.

The previous day, Matteo Bruni, Director of the Holy See Press Office, had said that the name Leo XIV referred to workers 'in the age of artificial intelligence'. 'Today, as in the time of Leo XIII, there is the problem of employment, because digitalisation is leading to a reduction in the necessary workforce', Cardinal Nemet stressed.

The Serbian cardinal also recounted a joke by the cardinals proposing 'another explanation' for the Pope's name: 'Until now we had Francis talking with wolves. Now we have a lion (*leone* means "lion" in Italian) who will hunt the wolves.'

For all that, Leo is no cowboy, as his American friends point out. The day after the election of the 267th pope, seven cardinal-electors from the United States gave a press conference at the North American College in Rome to make it clear that Robert Francis Prevost's stature went far beyond their country. Leo XIV 'is an American citizen, but he's also really a citizen of the whole world' who represents 'the big picture of the Church', said Cardinal Daniel DiNardo, Archbishop Emeritus of Galveston-Houston. 'Everyone says he's an American pope, but this man has spent most of his life in South America', emphasised Cardinal Christophe Pierre, Apostolic Nuncio to the United States. He also recalled the new pontiff's French origins and the mixed-race nature of his genealogy.

'I didn't feel that the conclave was a continuation of the American political elections', said Cardinal Wilton Gregory, assuring us that 'the concern of the cardinals was to find out who among us could bring us together' and spread the faith throughout the world. Cardinal Timothy Dolan added that Leo XIV 'reminds us that we all have our citizenship in heaven', and that his origin was 'an element of the past' 'Robert Francis Prevost is no more, he is now "Pope Leo", he is a new person, he is the Holy Father, he is the successor of Peter', he stressed.

American by birth, Robert Francis Prevost obtained Peruvian citizenship in 2015, when he was Bishop of Chiclayo, in northern Peru. Embodying this dual North American and Latin American identity, Leo XIV will therefore be a 'pontiff' in the truest sense of the word, building a bridge between two Americas whose relations have often been tumultuous.

The election of Cardinal Prevost to the See of Peter on 8 May 2025 has invalidated two criteria that might have seemed to rule him out from a geopolitical perspective. For a long time, the election of a pope from the United States had seemed impossible, given that country's weight in world affairs. The same applied to the election of a Latin American pope, after the 12 year pontificate of Argentina's Francis.

Robert Francis Prevost, by virtue of his origins, first and foremost embodies the concept of *métissage* [a fruitful cultural diversity], a reality that is only amplified by the acceleration of international mobility, and in which the Catholic Church is fully involved since its main axes of growth are linked to migration.

While most of the international media spontaneously noted the American nationality of the new Pope, the tone was different in Latin America, where the dominant headline in the press was: *El papa es Peruano* ('The Pope is Peruvian'). For Peru, marked by intense popular piety, the election of the Pope naturally represents a major event, 'a historic moment for the country and for the world', enthused Peruvian President Dina Boluarte.

'It's like winning the World Cup', said some Peruvians interviewed by the BBC in St Peter's Square. 'Peru is in a very complicated, very critical situation, but I think this is a message of hope for everyone', said one. 'We're happy and overwhelmed, because now we're famous for a while', another of the faithful confided to the British media. Cardinal Carlos Castillo Mattasoglio, Archbishop of Lima, expressed in a statement his 'enormous spiritual satisfaction' after this 'conclave experience' that led to the election of Pope Leo XIV, 'one of our own, who has become *achiclayanizado*', an untranslatable term expressing Robert Francis Prevost's integration into the local culture of Chiclayo.

Conclusion

So many challenges for one man. Leo XIV himself admitted that he was not up to the task. How could a mere mortal carry such an incalculably heavy load?

It was probably a secret between the Pope and God. A secret shared on the very day of the election, in the Room of Tears or perhaps in the Pauline Chapel. Fortunately, journalists do not have access to this reserved area.

But we have the right—and perhaps the duty—to speculate. Leo XIV was a man of prayer, a religious who knew what the interior life meant. We have it on good authority that this cardinal remained a religious. In Rome, he used to pray early in the morning, very early, deferring his many future decisions to someone beyond himself. As Pope, Leo XIV is unlikely to change his habits. Nothing is impossible for the one who believes, Jesus promises. And we have understood that the Bishop of Rome has a faith that can move mountains.

The peace he speaks of has nothing to do with a simple absence of conflict; it echoes the peace that the risen Jesus gave to his apostles. Our kingdom is truly not of this world, even if it begins here below.

Appendices

Divine Surprise

In the dictionary, the word 'surprise' has several definitions. It means 'the emotion caused by something unexpected'. It is synonymous with astonishment, amazement and sometimes even dazzlement. Surprise is also an action 'by which one takes or is taken unawares'; in other words, unexpected or unforeseen. In the long history of the papacy, there has been no shortage of surprises, the first of which is also a mystery: why did Jesus choose a fisherman from Galilee to build his Church, knowing that he would deny and betray him three times?

Indeed, the 'look' is surprising. Peter himself was not very proud of it. This can be seen from the Gospel of Mark, which Papias of Hierapolis, a 2nd century bishop, tells us was dictated by Peter himself. In this text, unlike the other three Gospels, Peter does not take pride of place. The Petrine charge is based exclusively on passages taken from the writings of Matthew, Luke and John. Peter had betrayed his master, and he knew that he had much to be forgiven. In Mark's Gospel, he therefore stands back and takes a step to the side in order to reveal his unworthiness.

However, this choice takes on its full meaning in the history of the Church as a whole, for two main reasons. The first is obviously the need for unity. Without Peter, Christianity is condemned to divide into so many chapels, churches and communities. The Johannine community, which wrote the very last chapter of the Gospel of Saint John, understood this well. When the apostle whom Jesus loved had just died, they realised that it was necessary for them to be attached to the chair of Peter. Hence the story of the miraculous catch of fish and the order Jesus gave Peter to govern his Church. Three times, as if to erase the three denials and therefore the imperfection of Simon Peter, Jesus asks him to feed his sheep.

This surprise in the choice of Peter tells us something else. Rather than relying on John, the one who remained at the foot of the cross, Jesus reminds us of the imperfection of human nature and therefore of what the Church will be in its history. Indeed, the Church would like a 'superhero' pope, as the Roman artist Mauro Pallotta put it in graffiti in a side alley near St Peter's Square, depicting Pope Francis at the very beginning of his pontificate, briefcase in hand and fist raised, flying through the air like Superman. But superheroes don't exist in the Church. There must be, so to speak, only saints, and not all popes are saints: far from it. So the election of a pope, then his very government, even his posterity, can be surprising in the truest sense of the word. Claudel put it this way: 'God writes straight with curved lines.'

The most obvious example is found in the Popes of the Renaissance. Our contemporary mentality does not conceive of the completely ludicrous idea that popes had 'quasi-conjugal' relationships. For example, Alexander VI Borgia (1492–1503) had at least five children by two different women! Yet he was unanimously elected on 11 August 1492, even though his foreign origins—he was Spanish—were against him. Yet, according to the *Historical Dictionary of the Papacy*: 'None of his contemporaries mentioned his immoral conduct or the existence of his children.' Contrary to the black legend of Alexander VI, the sources emphasise that he did not neglect his apostolic mission at all. Quite the contrary. He was the first pope to think of the Church on a global scale at a time when Christopher Columbus had just discovered the Americas. Pope Borgia also granted numerous privileges to religious orders and defended orthodoxy by stepping up the fight against heresy.

The same could be said of Pope Julius II (1503–1513), who had 'only' three daughters. An old opponent of Pope Alexander VI, Julius II, considered a sincere man, nevertheless duped the cardinal electors by haggling over his election. Unusually in the history of the Church, he was even elected in the first ballot! Nevertheless, Julius II is eternally associated with St Peter's Basilica as we know it today and with one of the greatest artistic geniuses in the history of mankind: Michelangelo. Julius II was also the symbol of resistance to the French crown, which wanted to get its hands on part of northern Italy. He thus appeared as the defender of the rights of the Holy See in the face of the emergence of modern states, as Pope Pius IX (1846–1878) and a certain Leo XIII (1878–1903) would later be against the Italian revolutionary and unitary process.

In this respect, the contemporary period of the papacy, from 1870 to the present day, has also been full of surprises, but of a different order. After the loss of the Papal States in 1870, the Papacy enjoyed a media centrality that it had never enjoyed before in history. The Pope, who considered himself a prisoner in the Vatican, aroused compassion throughout the world. The faithful, touched by this man trapped in the apostolic palace, came to his aid by contributing to the *Peter's Pence* collection, which was revived for the occasion. This pontifical centrality continued to grow over the decades until the era of the Internet, with the development of new means of communication (radio and television).

From then on, every new election, every word the Pope utters and every gesture he makes is scrutinised in a way that had never been the case before in the history of the Church. The surprises are all the greater. The choice of this or that cardinal, whether expected in the loggia or not, generates this effect of surprise, especially when it comes to the so-called 'compromise' candidates. Saint Pius X (1903–1914) was one of these. He came as a surprise because he did not speak the language of Vatican diplomacy, French. Unlike his predecessor, who came from a large Italian noble family, Cardinal Sarto came from a very modest family. Pius X put spirituality at the heart of his pontificate, abandoning the old political dream of recovering the Papal States lost in 1870. Contrary to popular belief, he brought the Church into the modern age by completely reforming the Curia and embarking on the task of re-writing canon law, which was thought to be impossible.

Elected in 1922 after fourteen rounds of voting, Pius XI was another candidate who, immediately after his election, caused a surprise that echoed round the world. While the popes still considered themselves prisoners in the Vatican and refused to leave the walls of Vatican City, Pius XI decided to bless the crowd from the basilica's famous loggia, a gesture that no pope had done for over 52 years! The sign was clear: the papal tiara had to be reconciled with the Italian crown. This was done with the Lateran Accords of 1929. Pius XI's policy was also surprising. He believed that the Bolshevik power would establish a regime of religious freedom. He also believed that negotiations with the German authorities were possible in the 1930s. This policy was, it has to be said, marked by naivety, even if it is a reminder of the Holy See's willingness to try whatever could be done, even when reaching out to the worst of regimes. Yet it was surprising in many ways, even to the point of causing silent suffering among the incredulous faithful.

And what of John XXIII, another pope of compromise, elected in 1958 after 11 ballots? Considered a transitional pope after the long pontificate of Pius XII (1939–1958), he turned the Church's relationship with the world on its head when, to everyone's surprise, he convened the ecumenical council of Vatican II. The idea had been mooted under previous pontificates but had been abandoned in view of the scale of the task. John XXIII, who was not in sufficiently good health to cope with such an event, asked that it be undertaken. He died in 1958, handing over the baton to Archbishop Montini, whose name had already been mentioned in the congregations that same year, even though he was not yet a cardinal. He was to become Pope Paul VI, which came as no real surprise. He himself did not weep in the famous Chamber of Tears.

The biggest surprise, of course, came when John Paul I died at the end of the summer of 1978, 33 days into his reign. Everyone wondered what message the Holy Spirit had wanted to send to the Cardinals: the field of possibilities was open. This allowed a pope from Eastern Europe to be elected after 8 ballots. John Paul II, too, was a compromise candidate. The cardinals' choice was a huge surprise because, for the first time since Adrian VI (1522–1523), a pope came from abroad. What was once a surprise became a habit, as no Italian had been elected as Peter's successor since 1978. The Polish pope was all the more surprising in many ways: he revolutionised the pontifical office by travelling to one hundred and twenty-seven countries and visiting no fewer than eight hundred cities. Above all, he was the only person in the Vatican to believe that the Soviet communist regime could not survive. The assassination attempt in 1981 did absolutely nothing to change his vision, despite his entourage putting pressure on him to abandon his fight against the Marxist hydra.

Pope Leo XIV was not a compromise candidate. Like several of his predecessors (Leo XIII, Pius XII, Benedict XVI . . .), he benefited from a rapid election that revealed the certainty of a choice. This means that the pre-conclave period played an important role in the rise of the American cardinal. This was no less of a surprise for many Vatican experts and religious commentators. Indeed, since the Great War, which enabled the United States to dominate the world, it had been customary to say that a North American cardinal could not be elected to the Chair of Peter. This was not the case. The surprise election of Cardinal Prevost revealed a personality that could not be confined to North America.

Born in Chicago to a French father and an Italian mother, Robert Francis Prevost spent most of his life in Peru. This polyglot thus embodied a form of cosmopolitanism that only the universality of the Church can offer. This choice came as no surprise to the one hundred and thirty-two cardinals who elected him.

Christophe Dickès,
Historian and journalist

Becoming One of Us and Disappearing in Christ

The first appearance of a newly elected Pope on the balcony of St Peter's is a moment that no one forgets. We scrutinise his gestures, his looks, his words. Who will he be? What will he be like? At a moment like this, what a godsend it would be if he himself told us who he is! 'I am a son of Saint Augustine': a religious of the Order of Saint Augustine, an Augustine (a term that many French speakers ignore and replace with 'Augustinian'), but also a disciple of Saint Augustine (354–430), someone who refers to the life, thought and spirituality of one of the most impressive giants of Christian history.

Then a phrase from this Saint Augustine comes to mind: 'With you I am a Christian and for you a bishop.' Here is a pope who, by means of a quotation, declares himself to be both for us and with us. He is above us, up there in his loggia, but he is also one of us, a Christian among Christians. To understand this better, let's go back to the ancient text.

For Augustine, it was the anniversary of his episcopal ordination. The memory of it lived on in him: he thought of it as if it were happening today. In his sermon (published by the specialists as number 340), he asked his people to pray for him, so that Christ would help him to carry the 'burden' that he had placed on his shoulders. The bishop confided in the crowd: 'It frightens me that I am here for you, but it comforts me that I am with you. For you, in fact, I am a bishop; with you, I am a Christian.' What is a Christian? Someone who has been saved. This comes before any particular mission and underpins everything else. Augustine goes on: 'I must rejoice more in having been redeemed with you than in having been placed at your head. Then, as the Lord asks, I will be more actively your servant, and I will not be ungrateful for the price he paid for me to be your companion in service.' Above all, Augustine saw himself as 'redeemed' by the same ransom as any other Christian. He and his diocesan colleagues are 'fellow servants' under the guidance of the One who paid the 'price' for their redemption. The bishop is the 'servant' of his people; they are all together in the service of the same Master.

On the evening of his election, immediately after quoting Saint Augustine, Leo XIV called on us to 'walk together towards this homeland that God has prepared for us'. By saying 'all together', by saying 'we', he in turn placed himself within the ecclesial logic embodied by the great bishop. He is not a monarch, not a star, not a superman, but one of us. He is not established, not installed, not achieved a destination, but he 'walks' with us towards the 'homeland' (a typical image of Saint Augustine) that is not of this world.

The Augustinian emphasis on the collective is reflected in the new pope's first homily, delivered in the Sistine Chapel on 9 May to the cardinals who had elected him the previous day. Speaking in one of the most fascinating places in the world, Leo XIV declared that the Church should attach less importance to 'the magnificence of its structures or the grandeur of its buildings' than to 'the holiness of its members'. That says it all. A decisive step backwards has been taken in the face of the infatuation of so many people, believers and non-believers alike, with what is sumptuous and spectacular about Catholicism in general and the papacy in particular. It is not a question of settling down firmly in this world and perpetuating the prestige of a powerful institution, but, as this homily goes on to say, of collectively, ecclesiastically, taking on 'the commitment of a daily journey of conversion'. The Augustinian spirituality of the new Pope consists in Catholics walking together, without respite, towards their Lord.

This individual and collective drive towards union with God for all eternity is not the idea of Saint Augustine alone, but is the deepest and most constant expression of the entire Christian tradition. This impetus comes through the total gift of self. So it is not surprising that the homily on 9 May (which deserves to be read over and over again) ends with a reference to another saint of antiquity: Ignatius of Antioch, a martyr. As he embarked on his new mission, Leo XIV knew perfectly well that, while the world's spotlight seemed to make him an international star, his vocation as Pope consisted, as he himself put it, in 'disappearing so that Christ might remain', in 'making himself small so that he might be known and glorified' in 'spending himself to the very end so that no one would miss the opportunity to know and love him'.

Augustinian because he was Christian, fraternal because he was paternal, in charge of us but resolutely among us, Leo IX had already explained to us in advance the meaning of his pontificate: he would gradually wear himself out and make himself transparent, the better to show the One he served.

Jean-Marie Salamito
Historian and university professor

Women and Governance

It is not easy to pinpoint Cardinal Prevost's views on the long-awaited question of the responsibility to be given to women, because he has said virtually nothing on the subject. Back in 2012, he is said to have coined the famous phrase taken up by Francis: 'We must not clericalise women.' While it may come as a surprise that he has not considered declericalising men, this pirouette suggests that he is not in favour of ordaining women.

On the other hand, at the last synod (2023–2024), he clearly showed his enthusiasm for the method chosen, that of 'walking together'. When we remember that this synod saw for the first time women with the right to vote, representing around 10% of the electorate, we can assume that he approves of this step forward.

His silence can be explained by the inflammatory nature of the subject. Indeed, the admission of women as decision-makers or dispensers of the sacraments is an essential marker between conservatives and progressives (an imperfect classification, but a real one). Thus, Burke is building a wall to oppose it, while Hollerich has made it known that he is in favour. As a prudent—and unifying—

man, Cardinal Prevost has therefore avoided committing himself too much on the subject, which does not mean that he does not have an opinion, nor that he does not feel free, now that he is Pope, to point out that Jesus never advocated the slightest differentialism, but that he considered everyone to be a human being of equal dignity.

Perhaps he will also recall that the question of women was the first to be put forward in the questionnaires submitted to Catholics by Pope Francis before the Synod, and that it is strongly supported by non-denominational opinion, by talented nuns in Switzerland and Germany, and by feminist associations throughout Europe.

To get a better idea of how things could evolve, it is useful to recall how the issue arose. In the Catholic Church, since the Gregorian reform (11th century), the responsibilities of *order* (sanctification of souls through the sacraments) and *government* (running a parish, a diocese, the Church as a whole) have been in the hands of ordained celibate men.

In his programmatic encyclical *Evangelii gaudium* (2013), Pope Francis called for this link to be relaxed: 'The reservation of the priesthood to males, as a sign of Christ the Spouse who gives himself in the Eucharist, is not a question open to discussion, but it can prove especially divisive if sacramental power is too closely identified with power in general.' (§104)

The pope has, in fact, decoupled order and government in two important areas: he has given women the right to vote, breaking with the previous discourse that kept them at a distance from public affairs, and he has appointed Simona Brambilla as Prefect—a responsibility previously granted only to cardinals—of the Dicastery for Institutes of Consecrated Life and Societies of Apostolic Life. Pope Leo XIV can therefore hide behind the overtures of Francis, by favouring governance over ministry.

It is almost amusing to note that the urgent need to find ways of empowering women is reviving and perhaps even accelerating the question of more collegial governance at the top.

There are several indications that Pope Leo was sensitive to this issue. He was a member of a religious order, accustomed to community life and collegial decision-making. We can assume that he would have the skill not to govern alone.

But above all, the problem had already been identified by Francis and was unable to be dealt with. Since 2013, however, it has become more acute. We can see in the dioceses, but also in Rome, that there is a lack of vital forces to govern well. In some Roman offices, the small number of people employed is impressive. Added to this is the pope's international aura. His moral authority must be based on sound diagnoses by the nuncios and curia staff, for example in terms of respect for people, education and the law in the various countries of the world. The pope will need more advice, from all categories of the faithful, as long as they are competent. At the same time, a subject related to governance is making a strong comeback: that of the unity of the Church. It is not so much a question of doctrinal unity as geographical unity. How can we claim to administer 1.4 billion faithful in the same way?

Pope Francis's decision to allow the blessing of homosexuals (*Fiducia supplicans*, December 2023) was met with a loud outcry from Africans, to the point that Francis had to admit the African exception. The facts speak for themselves!

There is an urgent need to recognise differences in discipline within the Church, to be dealt with according to the genius of each culture, at the discretion of continental Conferences. Have the cardinals given Cardinal Prevost a mandate to make progress in this area? If so, he would escape criticism from conservatives for wanting to sell off the unity of the Church, and a number of outstanding issues would find their solution there.

The emancipation of women and the globalisation of the Church are issues that early Christianity did not encounter. They could invite the new pope to 'widen the space of his tent' (Is 54:2)—a phrase he himself has taken up—towards new faces, new histories, new skills and new practices, which would make the Church imagined in a dream by a certain Hermas (*The Shepherd*, around 150 C.E.) a very old lady who knows how to grow younger.

–Anne Souper
Theologian and essayist

A Word of Enunciation

I note that this pontifical election is probably the one that has most excited the world of communication and political circles since the Second World War. How can this be explained?

First, because of the international crisis and the collapse of ideologies since the fall of communism. It is clear that many people are turning to religion to fill the void in this context of uncertainty.

Second, because of the personality of Pope Francis, who has unquestionably opened up new perspectives that echo this quest, and who has thus established himself as the first pope of globalisation. The question is whether his successor will be able to continue along this path. We will, of course, judge him by his actions. For the time being, our first impressions are still mixed. There are hints of a man of synthesis between different currents: a social orientation through his nod to Pope Leo XIII, a dimension of prudence too. And then, a form of cosmopolitanism with multiple roots, but dominated by a strong link with the world and Western history, more than with the global South. There was certainly his ministry in Peru, but he still belongs to the Old World more than the New.

Basically, everything depends on how we understand the function of the papacy in this complex international context. In the course of history, there have in fact been three different models.

For centuries, and even more than a millennium, the papacy played a major, but classic, diplomatic role. To do this, it had both conventional state support and a very strong moral and spiritual ascendancy over the reigning monarchs. In this sense, we could speak of a pontifical theocracy, which clearly became established during the medieval period, and which gradually gave way to a pontifical power that acted more or less discreetly, but genuinely, on temporal power and the diplomatic scene. Today, this old model is well and truly over, mainly due to the balance of terror. . . We remember Stalin's assassinating phrase: 'How many divisions does the Vatican have?' At times, the situation was even reversed, with state powers occasionally appealing to the Vatican for mediation, although the Vatican no longer played a coercive role.

A second model has emerged in modern times, particularly in recent decades: that of the 'influencer' pope. John XXIII, Paul VI and John Paul II played this card for all it was worth. The aim was to influence political behaviour and the choices of the faithful in order to influence the international game indirectly. This was clearly seen in the role played by John Paul II in the fall of communism in Poland and more widely in Europe. We are forced to recognise that this role is running out of steam, as a result of secularisation and the Church's loss of direct influence on people's consciences, but also because of a relaxation of traditional inter-state relations.

A third model is emerging, that of the papacy as an *enunciating* force. This is asserted through its ability to enunciate fundamental principles about the organisation of the world and relations between states. Pope Francis has fulfilled this role remarkably well, intervening on a number of important issues: immigration, as we saw in Lampedusa, the defence of the planet with the successful encyclical *Laudato si'*, and finally through the attempt to revive a humanist ethic. For Pope Francis, it was basically a question of humanising globalisation.

To make this notion of enunciation even more precise, I would say that it consists of formulating a word that transcends inter-state competition. To take a comparison, the pope's words are like those of international law, as pronounced by the International Court of Justice or the International Criminal Court: words that appear to be detached from the official inter-state game. This is not insignificant in our world: it is important for bodies to be able to say what is right, to recall the norms and the human dimension of this interdependent world, and to denounce unbearable situations from a metapolitical position, independent of the interests of power.

Will this approach, which Pope Francis has successfully adopted, survive his successor? It only works if the voice is loud enough. . . sometimes at the risk of a few slip-ups.

Bertrand Badie
Sociologist of international relations
Professor emeritus at the Institut politique de Paris.

www.ingramcontent.com/pod-product-compliance
Lightning Source LLC
Jackson TN
JSHW022339290625
86816JS00004B/23
* 9 7 8 1 9 2 3 3 8 5 4 2 9 *